John Franklin Cowan

A New Invasion of the South

Being a Narrative of the Expedition of the Seventy-first infantry...

John Franklin Cowan

A New Invasion of the South
Being a Narrative of the Expedition of the Seventy-first infantry...

ISBN/EAN: 9783744756914

Printed in Europe, USA, Canada, Australia, Japan

Cover: Foto ©ninafisch / pixelio.de

More available books at **www.hansebooks.com**

COLONEL RICHARD VOSE.

A NEW INVASION

OF THE SOUTH.

BEING A NARRATIVE OF THE EXPEDITION OF THE
SEVENTY-FIRST INFANTRY,
NATIONAL GUARD.

THROUGH THE

SOUTHERN STATES,

TO

NEW ORLEANS.

February 24—March 7, 1881.

By JOHN F. COWAN.

NEW YORK CITY,
BOARD OF OFFICERS SEVENTY-FIRST INFANTRY,
Publishers.

1881.

Dedicatory Note.

The expedition of the Seventy-first to the far South is an accomplished fact. It was thought that its significance was more than might appear at first sight ; that there was an underlying principle of greater import than the mere interchange of courtesies. This little book is published that the generous treatment of Northern men by Southern men may be known, and to commemorate an event, that it is hoped, by all who participated, will be but the forerunner of that era of national fraternity on which so much of the future of our great country depends.

To

ALBERT BALDWIN, Esq.,

President of the Royal Host, the narrative is dedicated with sincere esteem for him as a man and a citizen, by

THE AUTHOR.

TABLE OF CONTENTS.

TABLE OF CONTENTS.—Continued.

CHAPTER I.

A NEW INVASION.

"O Peace! thou source and soul of social life;
Beneath whose calm, inspiring influence
Science his views enlarges, Art refines,
And swelling commerce opens all her ports."
— *Thompson.*

TWENTY years ago the roar of a cannon on the shore of South Carolina proclaimed a fratricidal strife in America. The chain of brotherly love was broken. From Northern workshops and Southern fields went a million of men to end by force of arms what force of argument had failed to accomplish. The line of battle was drawn, and face to face stood brother and brother.

Twenty years ago the Seventy-first was one of the first organized regiments to offer its services to the National Government. For years the regiment had been distinctively called the American Guard, and its reputation was not unknown to the authorities at Washington. Its services were accepted. It is no part of the duty of the writer to tell the story of that conflict. It is written deeply enough in American soil. With that history the Seventy-first has indissolubly and most honorably interwoven its name and fame.

In 1861 it left its armory for the South. Strong men were moved and women wept as with steady ranks and grave faces the men marched down Broadway. The drums seemed to roll a funeral march. Many never came back—side by side with those who wore the gray--they lie in the sunny fields of the South. The flag was their shroud, the battle field their sepulchre.

In 1881 again the order came to march ; again there were the busy scenes at the armory; again the drums rolled out along Broadway. But it was no funeral roll this time, faces were smiling now, cheers and "God bless you's " took the place of tears and lamentations. The Louisiana regiments which had plunged into the fire and smoke of Bullrun to find the American Guard firm and steady amid the carnage, now waited with outstretched arms on the banks of the Mississippi, to welcome as brothers, those whom they had before met as foes.

In 1861 they met with crossed bayonets. In 1881 they met with clasped hands.

It was a new invasion of the South, but the olive and the magnolia twined about the rifles and the old flag rose and fell over all.

It was no mere frolic that took the Battalion of the

Seventy-first to the South. The men who formed the expedition were not idlers ; they did not enter into the expedition with idle motives. From the highest in rank to the drummer, they had occupation at home. They were in fact the peers of their fellow citizens who remained behind.

"With malice toward none," the Pelican had bowed its stately head to the Empire State and said :

"We of the South are anxious to show to you of the North that the war is over. The throbbing of the war drums is hushed, the rancor of the past is gone forever. The soldiers of the South are Americans like yourselves, they have been and are misrepresented by designing men, and they are tired of misrepresentation. The old sectional bitterness is swallowed up in the desire for a new era of peace and brotherly love. Come and visit us that we may show you how sincere we are."

And it was a mission of no slight import. Representative Southern men had issued the invitation. The Royal Host of New Orleans, probably the most powerful society in the Southern States, having for its object the developement of the financial and commercial interests of the South, and knowing no politics, no creed, headed the invitations with the offer of generous hospitality. The City of New Orleans, the State Government of Louisiana, the active National Guard and the veterans of the war joined in the tender of warm friendship. These offers of good will made the expedition a necessity. Its wisdom cannot be doubted, since the result is known. Hardly was the announcement made, when other States, Cities and towns wheeled into line and showered on the Battalion of the Seventy-first such an accumulation of honors as to raise the expedition to the dignity of National interest. Those who accompanied the expedition believed that the extraordinary reception accorded it on all sides and at every little hamlet *en route*, was a display of genuine feeling. The train bearing the blue coated soldiers of the North passed through many States, and it was nearest the heart of the old confederacy that the reception was warmest. No amount of dragooning for the sake of policy could have controlled the country sections of Kentucky and Mississippi. Yet there were hundreds of people who flocked about the stations and extended the right hand of fellowship, while there was not a single instance of unfriendliness. Thus it was that the men of the Seventy-first knowing that the eyes of the South at least were on them and with a heart-felt desire to meet the proffered friendship more than half-way, left New York, to return overwhelmed with kindness and hopelessly indebted to their hosts.

The 24th of February was a cold blustering day. The sun came out brilliantly enough in the morning but its rays were tempered with keen winds that searched every nook and corner for victims. The old armory was chilly notwithstanding the roaring fires that armorer Kennedy kept bright. Hundreds of men rushed about here and there preparing for a march that was to be memorable in the history of the regiment. Such an accumulation of blue noses and frosted ears it is probable, was never seen in the armory before. Young recruits listened to grey headed veterans as they told the story of the march of 20 years ago. The large garrison flag was flying from the roof and attracted attention from passers by. The wagons of the quartermaster gathered about the doors were being rapidly filled and there was altogether a scene of unusual bustle and activity. The order came to march, and the regiment filed out into the street and presented arms as the New Orleans Battalion marched past. There was a burst of melody from the band, and they were off down Broadway. The winds swept up from the lower bay with fierceness, and the themometer kept sinking until everything cracked. The sidewalks were crowded, nevertheless, and the regiment greeted with enthusiastic cheers. The music of the band died out by degrees, the musicians puffed and blew until their faces already red with the cold, became purple. Drum Major Jenks twirled his staff and fiercely pulled his mustache, and Bandmaster Joyce shook his cornet and swore till everything was blue. But it was of no use. The music was frozen !

The special train waited at the foot of Liberty Street. The engine was gay with flags and streamers, and the railroad officials were smiling. The last words were said, good-bys spoken, and the train was off. There was a grand series of salutes from two or three hundred torpedoes

that the railroad officials had taken care to place on the
tracks. The train moved away smoothly and swiftly, and
was soon far out of the sound of the enthusiastic cheers of
those of the Seventy-first who remained at home. Immediately behind the engine came the commissary and quartermaster's cars. Over the former commissary Jacob Hess
presided, and the myrmidons of Acting Quartermaster
O. C. Hoffman smashed the baggage in the latter. Following these, came three elegant passenger coaches, and
they were followed in turn by four palace cars. The leading car bore banners on either side. On one was incribed
"Seventy-first Regiment, *en route* New York and New Orleans." The other bore the legend :—Seventy-first New
York, Louisiana Tigers—1861-1881."

These banners proved a constant source of amusement
to the people along the route, and at every stopping place
were surrounded by a throng of gaping rustics. It took
about two hours for the boys to settle down. Each company was assigned a car, the officers and guests occupying
the others. Bandmaster Joyce, who was almost heart-
broken at his inability to get any music out of his band in
the march down Broadway, explained the matter by show-
ing how the instruments were frozen. Drum Major Jenks
on the contrary was in a high state of glee over the ef-
ficiency of the drum corps and the fact that the drums
could not freeze up. The Drum Major's elation, however,
was destined to be of short duration, for just before the
train reached Philadelphia he was seized with sudden and

mysterious cramps. Major Bryant and Hospital Steward Ingard took him in hand, and by the time Wilmington was reached, Jenks was himself again, and smiled cheerfully at the Wilmington girls, who gathered around to admire his gorgeous uniform.

There was no delay of importance and the train in due time reached Baltimore, but in the mean time the party had been entertained by the Commissary. When the train was about two hours out from New York, the companies were marched into one of the forward cars where a table had been arranged and a seat provided for each man. The *menu* comprised, besides coffee, excellent bread and butter, all sorts of pickles, cold turkey, chicken, ham, tongue, roast and corned beef, and it is needless to say that the boys did all they could in that direction, their good intentions being fortified by the long and cold march before embarking.

This programme was varied very slightly during the entire trip. Three meals a day were served on board the cars and coffee was picked up at certain stations. This was thought to be a better plan than depending on way stations. The stations however, were not entirely neglected, for many of the party were glad to snatch a warm meal now and again.

Baltimore was reached just as the shadows of evening were deepening. The train was boarded by a large delegation of gentlemen, who, making their way to the headquarter car, announced themselves as officers of the Fifth

Maryland. They were warmly received and while the train was being ferried across the river, pleasant little speeches were made, the first of the trip, by the visiting officers and several of Ours. The Marylanders brought with them a peculiar shaped box, which the Chaplain persists to this day in calling a "grain elevator." It certainly did look like one, the outside at any rate. It was said to be good grain too and to show a very high state of cultivation. As we crossed the river, the heavy booming of distant cannon was heard. "What is that?" everyone asked his neighbor. "It is the salute from Fort McHenry" we were informed. The booming grew more distinct as we neared the bank. It was almost quite dark and yet the outlines of the old fort were dimly seen, while from the ramparts there blazed the "loud mouthed advocates of war." Quickly it passed from car to car that the famous old fort was saluting us, where years ago it was asked :

"On that shore, dimly seen through the mists of the deep,
Where the foes haughty host in dread silence reposes
What is that which the breeze, o'er the towering steep,
As it fitfully blows, now conceals, now discloses?
Now it catches the gleam of the morning's first beam
In full glory reflected, now shines on the stream ;
'Tis the star-spangled banner ! Oh, long may it wave
O'er the land of the free and the home of the brave !"

The train halted and the band played the music of the grand old song, while the men cheered themselves hoarse in response to Captain J. G. Ramsay's and the Second U. S. Artillery's loud spoken compliments. The entire detachment regretted sincerely that night had fallen as a screen between it and the gallant battery.

CHAPTER II.

THE FIRST NIGHT OUT.

> " Most glorious night
> Thou wert not sent for slumber ! let me be
> A sharer in thy fierce and far delight, —
> A portion of the tempest and of thee !"
> —*Byron.*

> "Good Michael, look you to the guard to-night,
> Let's teach ourselves that honorable stop
> Not to outsport discretion."
> —*Shaks.*

THE first night out ! How its memories will imperishably cling to those who were on the train ! Baltimore was a thing of the past and even Bandmaster Joyce who had been waiting up to catch a view of Washington, consented to retire when the Capital City was forty miles in the rear. The train went through the city so quietly that only a favored few were permitted a sight of Pennsylvania Avenue, with its long vista of lights stretching far away into the gloom and the magnificent dome of the Capitol brilliantly shining with its myriad fires. One by one the weary soldiers sought their bunks—they thought—to sleep perchance to dream of future peaceful conquests. But alas! it was not to be. The combination of events on that night were too powerful to be resisted. Sleep was out of the question. To the wild spirits on board, nature lent aid and hardly were the sports of man completed ere the elements played havoc with the hours of darkness that remained. When the train left Jersey City, guards were regularly mounted, and the usual officers of the day and guard assumed charge of the welfare of the party. In the officers' car there was a choice quartette. Mr. C. K. Lord, General Passenger Agent of the Baltimore and Ohio Railroad, is a gentlemen whose face and physique denotes the happy traits of character he possesses in an eminent degree. Full of fun and good humor and withal a railroad official of ability, he made friends of all whom he met during his short stay with the train. Mr. Charles P. Craig, General Eastern Passenger Agent of the same line was almost a counterpart of Mr. Lord save as to physique. Mr. Frank Marsh, General Eastern Passenger Agent of the Jackson route, was as genial and attentive as a man could well be, and he and Mr. Craig, both of whom accompanied the party on the entire trip, became exceedingly popular

"SHOW YOUR TICKET."

with both officers and men. The fourth spirit of this quartette, was Mr. Theodore Lee, manager of the American Bank Note Company. He was as natty and bright as one of his own bank notes, and his wit and good fellowship were as clean cut as are the steel engravings of the institution with which he is connected. These gentlemen, not without help however—contrived to set the ball rolling. Everyone on the train was trying his best to sleep, when Lord and Lee got thirsty. The "Spirit of the 5th Maryland" was safely tucked away in the Surgeon's department, and as it had been announced that Dr. Bryant slept with a lancet in each hand, they did not think it altogether advisable to awaken him. After a solemn consultation in the end of the parlor car, they determined to consult Craig. He grumbled a little, but got up and joined the plotters. They looked about for a victim. A sonorous snore came from Marsh's bunk. It was startling in its distinctness, and seemed to suggest something to Craig. The conspirators adjourned to the platform, and Craig unfolded his plan. Then Lee and Lord went into a corner, lighted cigars and awaited developments, while Craig went to look for the officer of the day. That official was dozing in a forward car.

"Captain" said Craig solemnly, "there is a man in the officers' car, who has no ticket and does not belong to the regiment."

"Better wake up quarter-master Hoffman."

"He looks like a very decent man!"

"Perhaps there is some mistake. Better call up Colonel Vose and consult him. I do not want to put a man off at this time of night and such a night" continued the officer of the day drawing his cloak around him with a shiver as the snow flakes flew past the window.

"Well, I think he ought to be seen to" insisted Craig.

"Come along then" said the officer, and the two men went into the car where the other conspirators had turned down the lights, and stood awaiting the denouement. Marsh was sleeping the sleep of the just railroad man. His face was wreathed in peaceful smiles—at least it was so thought, it being too dark to ascertain such facts absolutely.--nothing but an occasional gentle sigh was heard from the location where his form, dimly outlined in a blanket, was seen. In a moment his rest was over, for the hand of the officer fell heavily on his shoulder, and a hoarse voice sounded in his ear !

"Where is your ticket, and how did you get on this train."

"Go away and let me sleep" he mumbled, turning over and taking a new grip on the side of the bunk.

"You must wake up and show me your ticket."

"Oh go to the deuce, and let me be," said the unfortunate man.

"Sergeant, bring a file of men here," was the next thing. Craig almost betrayed himself at this point by choking violently, and Lee and Lord had to go out on the platform notwithstanding the storm, in order that their screams might be lost amid the howling of the winds. The men came—Marsh was hauled out and his identity discovered to the astonishment of the men when a lantern was held to his face. The officer of the day arrested the entire party, and took them into the Commissary's car where numerous baskets of wine were stored. It was their opportunity and Marsh opened a number of bottles. Then Craig went to bed and fell asleep, and the arch conspirators, Lee and Lord went into executive session again. After matters had quieted down, Marsh went to the Quartermaster and gravely informed him that there was a disreputable man on board who had no ticket! The Quartermaster was of course highly indignant and went to the officer of the guard, as the officer of the day had gone to sleep. That official went in and performed the same ceremonies with Craig, that his superior had with Marsh, and the latter was by no means an uninterested spectator. Craig had to get up and on the usual adjournment to the Commissary's car, opened what was left of a case of Jules Mumm. In the morning the story was told to the few that did not know it, and was considered an excellent joke. It was not fully appreciated however, until the announcement was made that it had been a basket of Colonel Vose's private stock that had gone down the throats of the conspirators and the guards. It cost the railroad men more than a basket, to set matters right. It was long after midnight when the revels thus began, ended.

Leaving Baltimore, the train was nearly three hours behind time owing in part to delay in starting, and partly to a detention at Philadelphia, where the tracks of the Baltimore and Ohio crossed those of the Pennsylvania road. It was decided to make up this time before reaching Cincinnati. On this side of the Alleghanies, the train was met by a heavy snow storm which more or less delayed the ascent. The best engine on the road was put on the train at the summit, and "Chickahominy" was given charge of her. The engineer was given the name because of some daring experience he had had at that battle, and whatever that experience may have been "Chickahominy" will linger with us forever as the synonym for boldness in locomotive driving.

When everything was ready for the downward trip, Mr. Lord went forward and said a few words to the engineer. There was a hurried consultation of railroad officials and the signal to start was given. "Chickahominy" tried his valves, looked forward into the driving snow; blew an unearthly whistle and opened the throttle. We were off! The whistle was like the wail of some monster, plunging into a bottomless abyss. Faster fell the snow and faster flew the heavy train. It was well that few of the party really knew the horrors that encompassed them. On either side were mountainous caverns, in the far depths of which could they have seen the giant trees were dwarfed to insignificence. Through tunnels, over bridges, around curves, we plunge with frightful speed and—

"Mountain on mountain exultingly throws
Through storm, mist and snow its bleak crags to the sky."

It was an awful ride, down those mountains. The pace grew faster as the moments passed, until no one could sleep.

" Fifty miles an hour" whispered one railroad man to another.

" Yes and getting faster," was the response.

" Its sixty now " was said in less than five minutes, and the men closed their watches, and with close knit brows, held firmly to the nearest support. The great sleeping coaches made lurches now and again that prevented any-one from staying in bed. Everything movable was thrown about, and the pitching was like a ship in a heavy sea. Very many of the party were sea-sick, and all were ready for the final lurch which seemed to approach with every curve. Swaying from side to side, flying through space, the train sped on. There was no slaking, no uncertainty about it. Every man realized that when "Chickahom-ny " had opened the throttle valve, he intended to make the fastest run on record. He was the man to do it, and he did it. He knew that every approaching curve might be his last, but he also knew that the track had been cleared ahead, and that he was responsible for nothing but the speed of his train. Down and further down the moun-tains we plunged, over a grade of 125 feet to the mile, and nothing could be heard but the howling of the wind and intermingling with it, an occasional exulting shriek from the engine as some mountain station whisked by. As the first break of day chased the gloomy shadows and showed the rocky passes through which we whirled, all covered with a snowy fleece, the final lurch came. With the roar of a wounded lion, the engine slakened and stopped, all smoking and panting like some high bred steed, that had done its best devoir, and awaited the plaudits of the crowd. "Chickahominy" wiped his brow, lighted his pipe and got down from the foot board all white and nervous, like a man who had passed through the ordeal of a lifetime. The boys of Ours flocked about the iron monster, and with a soldiers disregard of dangers passed, laughed and joked.with each other. The snow ceased falling, and the sun came out. "Chickahominy" had done his duty. We were on time to the minute!

CHAPTER III.

A CINCINNATI WELCOME.

Whoe'er has travelled life's dull round,
Where'er his stages may have been,
May sigh to think he still has found
The warmest welcome at an inn.

—*Shenstone.*

They eat, they drink, and in communion sweet
Quaff immortality and joy.

—*Milton.*

WHEN the Delaware river was crossed, the men thronged the windows and platforms of the cars, and shouted "where is George, oh where is George!" Several natives who stood about the train, and who evidently bore the first name of the father of his country, blushed with conscious pride, and stood out in bold relief, as if to say "there may be a number of George's about here, but if you refer to *the* George, why here I am". The boys continued to shout however for "George" with an occasional addenda of "Wash," until the river was far in the stern. The ice was there, the flat boat was there, but the figure of the General was wanting. The remembrances of the crossing of the Delaware seemed to linger with the party, and so when the whistle blew for Cincinnati, the platforms were filled again, and the boys began to ask for the pigs.

"Where are the pigs?" asked one, of a laborer who was standing near the track, as the train drew up at the station.

"In the cars bedad!" was the ready response.

If the pigs of Cincinnati were not seen in great numbers in the streets, the mud upon which their fellow creatures thrive in the North certainly was. There was mud everywhere. The First Regiment of Infantry, Ohio National Guard, was found waiting at the depot. They were uniformed in the old United States fatigue, and one effect of our visit, was a movement on the part of the city to properly uniform this command. They deserve recognition, for they marched well and were a steady and soldierly body of men. They were, of course, muddy and so were we after marching 15 minutes. At Cincinnati, we were to leave the Baltimore and Ohio, and take the Ohio and Mississippi and Jackson routes for the far South. A perfect swarm of railroad men came down on us at Cincinnati. With the combination of talent that interested itself in our behalf, it was really a remarkable thing that the train escaped entire destruction. A list of a few of them may not prove uninteresting at this point, for it was at this point that we began to realize that we were utterly helpless in the hands of these men. Frank Marsh had recovered his usual good spirits, notwithstanding the severe dressing down that he, Craig and Lee had received from the Colonel for their escapade of the last chapter, and Marsh had some reason to be in good spirits. Were we not to be on the great Jackson route in a few short hours, and consequently at his mercy? But to return to the other railroad men who were flying about, giving orders, and consulting as to the probability of our colliding with the Swamptown express at Pohasket, or some other train somewhere else. There were of course C. K. Lord and Charles P. Craig who were almost in tears, because we were obliged to change from the "B and O Sleepers" to the comparatively crude and uncomfortable "Pullman's;" there was Marsh, happy as a Mississippi pilot, astride of a snag, running around with his hands full of telegrams; there was Thomas P. Barry of the Marietta and Cincinnati railroad, otherwise known as the "Parkersburg route," who was urging on some of the officers the superiority of Cincinnati whiskey to that of Baltimore; there was Mr. C. S. Cone, Jr., General Passenger Agent of the Ohio and Mississippi road, and his friend Mr. S. Horace Goodin, both of whom accompanied us further South, and made many friends among our party; there was William Murray, who in his august person, represented

three railroads at New Orleans; J. E. Rose, Master of
Transportation, Marietta and Cincinnati route ; William
Clements, Master of Transportation, of the Baltimore and
Ohio road, who was regarded with reverence as the man
under whose direction we had been almost sacrified to
" time " in coming over the Alleghanies ; William West of
the Marietta and Cincinnati road, whose courtly demeanor
when counting the detachment, was the admiration of all
observers, and three or four others whose names are not
at hand.

All this time the First Ohio, was standing patiently in
the mud, and the boys of Ours in their dress uniforms,
were forming the battalion, while everybody stood in the
way. The police arrangements of the city were about as
bad as the mud, but the policemen were anxious enough
to do something for us. . It was probably in the strength
of that desire, that they would occasionally whack some
inoffensive looking specimen of humanity that viewed the
procession open mouthed. The First Ohio was still in
the mud as we passed out of the depot and waded towards
it. Colonel Hunt presented arms, and Ours went by at
three-quarters speed. Then we made fast to the bank,
and the First paddled by us in column of fours, in single
rank. They seem to take most kindly to the column of
fours in single rank all through the South. The sidewalks
were literally packed with men, women and children, who
were not particularly enthusiastic, but treated the men
with great kindness nevertheless. After the usual formal-

ities, the line of parade was taken up. The two regiments marched through Elm to Fourth Street, eastward to Vine, northward to Seventh, westward to Central avenue, northward again to Fifteenth, eastward to Elm, southward to Court, through Race to Eighth, and Walnut to Fifth. The line of march was crowded with ladies and gentlemen. At almost every corner the houses were decorated, and on a prominent point at Fourth Street, an arch was erected, bearing the words, "Welcome to the Seventy-first." After the parade, arms were staked on the Esplanade, and the battalion was entertained at dinner at the Gibson House.

This dinner at the Gibson House was rather a pleasant affair, though somewhat hurried. There were no speeches. There was no time for that sort of thing. The dining-room in the Gibson House is a spacious one, and in many ways, well fitted for a public dinner. Tables were laid in long rows, with some at right angles in one end of the room. At one of these sat Colonels Hunt and Vose in stately grandeur, neither of them daring to eat much, and both more or less famished. The men occupied the other tables and rattled the china in feeble imitation of Jenks and his motley "Krewe." There was very little time after dinner, and a portion of that was to be devoted to a parade. So everyone hurried away in quest of barber shops, cigar stores and similar institutions. A small but exceedingly select company hunted up an accident insurance office, and exclaimed in a body :

"We want to get insured !"

The clerk looked in a bewildered way at the uniforms, and shook his head sadly.

"Wha—what do you mean?" was the next shout.

"When does the fight come off?"

"Oh 'come off' yourself" said an irreverent private in the rear, whereupon the clerk retired and his place was taken by a higher official, who smiled blandly at the tableau of gold lace before him.

"You want accident insurance tickets gentlemen? Certainly. I shall be obliged to charge a small increase on our regular rates, because of the circumstances you know—fast special train and all that sort of thing you know—"

The tickets were procured, and the party departed very much pleased. "My wife told me the very last thing" said one of the party, to get an insurance ticket for $1,000. 'Because' said she, 'you know dear, that no one ever gets killed who is insured, and if an accident should occur, how much more pleasant it would be to think that you would be cared for!'"

The parade to the depot of Ohio and Mississippi road was almost a repetition of the march to the hotel, except that the throng of sight-seers had increased and it was almost impossible to press through. The police had evidently never seen such a thing as a military parade, and it never occured to them that the First Ohio and the Seventy-first were anything but a sort of second class circus show. We marched in column of companies and only about ten files front at that, but could not preserve the

CINCINNATI MUD.

formation for half a block because of the wagons, cars and people that crowded the street and blocked the way. After everything was ready and the procession was under way, it appeared something like this :

Mud.

Eighteen Small Boys.

Six Policemen,

(Out of Step with the Music.)

Colonel Hunt and Staff,

Baker's Wagon and Two Little Girls.

Mud.

Band of the First Ohio.

One Street Car drawn by a Mule.

One Man distributing Circulars of a Pain Eradicator.

First Company, 1st Ohio.

Second Company, 1st Ohio.

One Policeman, evidently lost.

Third Company, 1st Ohio.

Delegations of Citizens on foot.

Two clean Street Cars and

One Dirty Butcher's Cart.

Drum Major Jenks.

Mud.

Band of the 71st.

Colonel Vose and Staff.

First Company, 71st.

Mud.

Second Company, 71st.

Three Brewer's Wagons.

Third Company, 71st.

Delegation of Citizens in Carriages—more or less full.

Fourth Company, 71st.

More Mud.

Promiscuous Citizens.

The parade was continued to the depot, and the cars boarded amid cheers. The courtesies shown the party by the First Ohio were thoroughly appreciated, and a feeling of great friendliness sprang up between the men. The Cincinnatians left nothing undone to make our stay a pleasant one, and notwithstanding some little drawbacks, already referred to, the men retain very pleasant memories of the city.

CHAPTER IV.

EGYPTIAN HOSPITALITY.

> "Away down South in Dixie,
>   Look away! look away!
> Away down South in the land of cotton,
> Cinnamon seed and sandy bottom,
>   Look away! look away!
> Away down South in Dixie!"

CINCINNATI was far away before morning. The second night was a quieter one than the first, and most of the men slept well. In that connection, it is not more than fair to say that the sleeping arrangements were excellent during the entire trip. The cars were commodious, and the men who did not take sleeping berths, could make themselves very comfortable. Those who did prefer to go to bed were furnished by the quartermaster with a ticket like this :

Sleeping Car, No................

LOWER BERTH.

Section No................

Mr...

71ST REGIMENT SPECIAL TRAIN.

Just what those tickets were for, was something " no feller could find out " although it was surmised that they meant something, because the quartermaster came through the train just before it reached New Orleans, and asked to see the " sleeping checks. " He only saw about half of them, because the other half had been torn into little square checks for some mysterious purpose, but he seemed just as well pleased as if he had got them all. The evening was a most pleasing one to those of the party who gathered in one of the cars, for there a sextette of the band played a varied selection of popular and operatic music, while a number of singers and speakers filled in the time allowed the musicians to fill up with wind and spirits—"of the Fifth Maryland." The train rolled steadily during the night, and in the early morning Cairo was announced to be in sight. It is a forlorn place in every sense of the word. Lying on a tongue of land protruded between the Ohio and the Mississippi rivers which unite just below it, it should be a garden of flowers. It is almost a barren waste of mud, but it is a picturesque place nevertheless, dirty and scrawny as it is. Straggling lines of unkempt houses in the background, a fringe of naked trees along the river front, and a few flat bottomed steamboats puffing here and there—such is this once famous military depot. The cars had to be taken from the tracks here, and put on others of a wider guage. This was rather a tedious business, although the master of the workmen swore and raved at them until the very jackscrews looked askance. When the cars were ready, they were rolled on an enormous ferryboat to cross the Ohio into Kentucky. The boat was a peculiar looking thing, if anything more ugly and unweildy than the Maryland that plies our waters at home, and carries cars between Jersey City and Morrisania. But she was well handled and stemmed the muddy current bravely for Egypt's shore.

There was a man in Cairo who kept a huckster shop. To him was intrusted the duty of providing coffee for the party. He had never probably seen so large a party of coffee drinkers, and his sympathies were evidently not with the "Yanks." He was the only man in the whole Southern trip that the writer wanted to kill, and he don't know but he may re-visit Cairo at some future time for that purpose. He did not only give us bad coffee, but he soured it with such an ungracious manner and surly speech, that had an alligator crawled out of his native mud and swallowed him, coffee, alleged sugar and all, it would

have been a pleasing sight—but a very disagreeable thing
for the alligator no doubt.   Shakespeare in the Comedy
of Errors, describes this man—or another just like him as
follows :

"They brought on Punch, a hungry, lean-faced villian,
A mere anatomy, a mountebank,
A threadbare juggler and a fortune-teller,
A needy, hollow-eyed, sharp looking wretch,
A living dead man:"

Peace to his ashes !

Egypt presented little hope of breakfast, though it was
said that far down the track, there were several houses
where "something" might be purchased.   The men and
officers scattered to forage,   The writer and one or two
others found a place where the smiling housewife said
that she could and would prepare a meal at 25 cents a
head.   Never was a breakfast more enjoyed, and there is
not a man of the 20 that sat down but remembers the
Egyptian hospitality with thankfulness.   The fare was as
follows :

Genuine Kentucky Bean Coffee,
(Much better than it sounds.)
Hoe Cake.
Ham and Eggs.
Hominy.
Real Milk.
Very good Butter and Bread.
Pork Steaks and Fried Potatoes.
Pickles and Apple Sauce.

Other houses opened their doors to the hungry soldiers
and many a face that frowned when leaving Cairo, was
wreathed in smiles when the whistle blew for a departure

from Egypt, for the memory of hog, hominy and hoe cake lingered with the men. There was a ruinous old barrack building near the railroad that interested the party very much. All this section of country was at one time covered with regiments, and some of the veterans of Ours had passed over the ground in the days gone by. The only wonder was how they could have lived on such a peculiar soil. The ground was swampy and the low banks of the river were everywhere overflowed. The flat bottom steamboats attracted more than ordinary attention, and much chaffing was indulged in between the coffee-colored deck hands and the boys of Ours. Several old darkies stood about the cars and asked questions, seemingly much interested in the uniforms. Two officers approached a house standing back a short distance from the river, more from curiosity than anything else. Three or four little pickaninnies were playing before the door. One of the officers called the youngest of the boys to him, and patting him on the head, asked him his name and age. The little fellow hung down his head and ran away confused. Just at this moment his mother, a woman of fifty or thereabouts, opened the cabin door. In a moment she appeared to appreciate the situation.

"Granville Jackson you come right hyar and be spectful to the gemmen. Dey is Yank hossifers you 'ittle brack fool and is used to bein' spected." Granville Jackson however, continued to hang his head and remained at a safe distance.

" How do you know we are officers ? " the mother was asked.

"I golly, I reckon I know hossifers when I see 'em, Used to see right smart of 'em 'bout hyar 'fore the surrender."

" How did you know we were northeners ? "

" Knowed that for suah, Colonel, 'cause everybody 'bout hyah was saying dot de Yanks was a comin.' I used to live right over hyar on a place. Is dey hard times in de north since the surrender? Find it pretty hard 'bout hyar, can't do much no way."

It was evident at Egypt that we were really in Dixie. The whole aspect of affairs changed. The firemen of locomotives were darkies as were also the brakemen. The conductor of our train was a genuine specimen of one type of a Southener, and everything seemed strange and new. Attention was called to the fact that we were now really in the South ; that we were there as guests ; that the people were hosts, and that the men should not for a moment forget these things. The orders issued by the Colonel were most cheerfully obeyed and there was not a single instance of a breach in that direction.

The wintry aspect of our Northern landscape remained practically unchanged, but the country differed widely from the North in the sparseness of its settlement, and a certain air of lack of capital which seemed to envelope it down to the flowers and birds of the Pelican state. As away the train sped along, through miles of low and swampy

ground, a peculiar type of Southern life was made mani-
fest. For miles the inhabitants were chiefly negroes who
tenanted log cabins, one story high, with chimneys of logs
and plastered with mud. The occupants generally owned
from one to four acres of land, on which they raise cotton
enough to support them in their simple mode of life from
season to season. This year the crop was both poor and
and backward, owing to the severe winter. In many fields
men and women were observed picking the cotton flower.
Our train made few stops, but whenever we did draw up
at a station, we found a throng of men, women and children, white and black, whose demonstrations were most
friendly. As the distance from Egypt was made longer,
a marked change in the country was observed, and the
climate grew milder. We were passing from winter into
spring. The woods and fields gradually put aside their
wintry aspect, and the budding leaves and foliage fortold
our approach to summer land. At Milan, Tennessee, the
train stopped for dinner, after which most of the detachment lounged about the platforms, and talked with the
throng of people gathered to do us honor. A little darkey, black as a coal, and as lively as a rat, addressing one
ot the men asked :

"Be you a Yankee ?"

"Oh, no" was the response "I am a New Yorker."
The boy's face grew very thoughtful. His eyes rolled
wildly. He looked dejected and inquisitive. A Yankee
he knows. But his whole being embodies itself in an in-

terrogation mark, and seems to ask : "What on earth is a New Yorker?" Oh, Emperial city of Manhattan Island, crowned with trophies, and lassoing the corners of the earth to thy feet with thy railroads and telegraphs, and white sailed ships! Even thy name and fame have limitations. There are those to whom thy mighty name is but a meaningless sound. Never having seen a genuine plantation dance, a party soon formed a ring around this same diminutive darkey, whose raiment, scanty even in its original shape, seemed about to leave him altogether. The little fellow shook it down right merrily, executing some movements that would make our "variety specialists" turn green with envy. He was rewarded with a handful of nickels—probably untold wealth to him, and when the train departed, stood looking after it with wide extended eyes as if a vision of paradise was passing from him.

CHAPTER V.

MISSISSIPPI AND LOUISIANA.

> O beauteous Peace!
> Sweet Union of a state! what else but thou
> Gives safety, strength and glory to a people?
> — *Thompson.*

HOLLY SPRINGS is only a short distance over the Mississippi border. A signal was flying there for the train to stop, and stop it did. Hundreds of people crowded about the little station, ladies waved their handkerchiefs from the windows and balconies, and a line of soldiers in gray, were drawn up at present arms. They were the Autrey Rifles, and were paraded in our honor. The men were turned out and drawn up in a long line without arms, and everybody awaited developments. Presently a tall and commanding looking man forced his way through the crowd, and bared his head. There was a hush at once. Colonel Vose made his way up the line, and stood near while a number of officers grouped themselves about the two. It was Major General Winfield Scott Featherstone, at one time commanding a Division in the Southern Army, and he addressed us on behalf of the State of Mississippi and the citizens of the County. The General said :

"I welcome you across our border. There was a time when your coming would have occasioned a feeling of fear and distrust ; that was in the bitter past. Thank God it has passed! (Cheers.) The North and the south never understood one another ; never had a grand convocation until 1861, when the country was in arms from the Atlantic to the Rio Grande. Thank God those days are gone. We welcome you here. We want you to see our people and our fertile soil. All we need now is capital. Your coming will do much to make us acquainted. You will find us of the South, as loyal to our country's flag as you are. (Enthusiastic cheers.) When the time comes for our great country to have a foreign war and we can never have any other, we will march with you against our common enemy. The Seventy-first New York, will march side by side with the Seventy-first Mississippi, under the same officers, and the same flag, for our cause and our country are one."

Colonel Vose responded, thanking the General for his kindly words, and assuring him, that when the moment came, the soldiers of New York would be found ready to march shoulder to shoulder with those of Mississippi to Victory. Then there arose such a yell from the Mississippians as few of the boys of Ours had heard in many a day. It was the old "war yell" given with a vim, and redoubled when the band struck up Dixie and Yankee Doodle. The cheer of the regiment mingled with the prolonged, piercing cry, and the strains of the band were almost lost. General Featherstone stood with his head uncovered, his long white locks flowing in the wind, his face full of animation and fire, the very beau ideal of the *ancien regime.* Colonel Vose stood beside him, his long military cloak thrown back, his head erect and features smiling, the beau ideal of a soldier. Their hands were clasped. The whole tableau was spirited and dramatic— the long line of blue uniforms, the smoking train, the gleaming rifles of the boys in gray, the hundreds of anxious, curious faces peering over their shoulders, made a picture that the golden shadows of the deepening twilight exquisitely framed. It was one of the most interesting episodes of the entire trip. The warmth and spontaniety of the greeting made us feel that we were among brothers indeed.

A few miles more and we had run into a thunder shower—remember, this was in February—the lightning flashed vividly, and the rain fell in torrents far into the night. The boys did not care much for that however, as they were comfortable enough in the cars, and thought that:

> The poet may talk of his lutes and guitars,
> Or screw up his fiddle of sorrow;
> But while we have plenty of pipes and cigars,
> We'll look for a brighter to-morrow.

From a heavy snow storm, to a warm thunder shower in forty-eight hours, was something of a change, but the boys did not spend the night in pondering over it by any means. Many a quiet way-side station that night, echoed with the regimental cheer, which by the way, became very popular in the South, and many requests were made for its repetition when once heard. It runs, as near as it can be expressed in print, as follows:

> Hurrah! Hurrah! Hurrah!
> Seventy-one! Seventy-one! Seventy-one!
> Rah! Rah! Rah!
> S-sssssssssssss!
> Boom! Ah!-h-h-h-h!!

Sunday morning broke bright and beautiful, and when the train pulled up in Hammond, Louisiana, it was like a June day. The flowers were in bloom, the trees were green; and the darkies were running about with very little more on than was provided by nature. The large hotel looked inviting, and many a pair of lips were smacked in anticipation of a good breakfast, for it was announced that here we were to meet a company of uniformed men from Buffalo, and that we should consequently be delayed for about two hours. The hotel was invaded, but alas! the Washington Artillery detachment had stopped there over night, and had eaten the hotel people out of house and home! The detachment numbered only about fifty men, but the hotel man said that he had never seen such eaters in his life. This same detachment welcomed us with a royal salute from field pieces brought up with them from New Orleans the night before. They served the guns magnificently. Every man in the detachment was a veteran of the war, and a gentleman of business and social prominence. Their coming so far to meet us, was esteemed by the men of Ours as a compliment of the highest order. Many and graphic reminiscences were interchanged between the veterans of both sides. One of the artillerymen said that he had a bullet in him somewhere —a yankee bullet—and if he could only get it out, he would present it to one of Ours, whereupon one of our veterans declared with tears in his eyes, that he had a piece of a Johnny bullet in his thigh, and that he would give a thousand dollars to get both of them out so they could exchange. Then the two veterans went off to get a drink, and everybody within hearing, wished that they had a bullet in some portion of their body. Colonel Horton of the Washington Artillery in a few words, referred to the fact that his regiment and the Seventy-first had exchanged leaden compliments a number of times, and a committee of the army of the Tennessee presented our boys with a handsome silk banner, bearing words of cordial welcome and greeting.*

But, while all this was going on and most of the party were drinking champagne and eating cold sandwiches, a small number of very hungry men were skirmishing for

*Appendix E.

a breakfast. Things were beginning to look very blue, when a gentleman came forward and tendered the hospitalities of his house. This was Mr. C. E. Cate, one of the most genial and pleasant men the detachment encountered on the trip. Mr. Cate insisted, and the party made but a feeble show of resistance. His handsome little Villa was situated about a quarter of a mile from the depot, approached by paths shaded with rustling leaves and flanked with perfumed hedges. The party was ushered into the parlor and presented to Mrs. Cate. We then realized how genuine the desire was, to show us true hospitality. This gentleman was known to none of us; he was in no way connected with, or responsible for our reception. He only knew that we were Northeners, the guests of Louisiana, and consequently of his. His whole manner was a courteous and kind reminder that we were welcome to the sunny South and the sunny hearts of its people.

View them near
At home, where all their wealth and pride is placed;
And there, their hospitable fires burn clear."

It was the first instance of the trip where any of the party had been invited to the home of a Southern gentleman; it was only the beginning of a round of social attention that was unprecedented in the history of any body of travelers.

The train started at last for the Crescent City, fifty miles distant. The organization already referred to, had arrived, and their train followed ours. With us went the Washington Artillery, and a special car containing a couple of cannons and innumerable bottles of wine. The fifty miles ride along the river was the most interesting portion of the trip. The scenery was entirely new to most of the party. The cabins and houses had a ruinous look. Every now and again, the train whirled by the ruins of a cotton press, at one time no doubt, the busy centre of a great plantation. The soil was under cultivation; men were busy plowing the fields that were not under water. The woods presented an appearance of dense tropical undergrowth, surmounted with cotton-wood trees, mossy and weird-like in their gaunt nakedness. Along the banks of the river were dense groves of the Sycamore, intermingling with the Southern pine, all in leaf, their roots and trunks washed by the overflowing Mississippi. Then an orchard whisked by, the trees in blossom, the perfume permeating the cars, and together with the Magnolia and Orange freighting the soft and balmy air with incense until the senses were beguiled to dreaminess, only to be roused by the sharp whistle for New Orleans.

CHAPTER VI.

.

IN THE CRESCENT CITY.

Monarch of heroes in the wide domain
Where Freedom writes her signature in stars,
And bids her Eagle bear the blazing scroll,
To usher in the reign of peace and love,
Thou mighty Mississippi!   *   *   *
        It reigns alone!

Aye gather Europe's royal rivers all—
Our Mississippi, rolling proudly on,
Would sweep them from its path, or swallow up,
Like Aaron's Rod, these streams of fame and song!
                            —*Hale.*

THE arrival in New Orleans was of course the feature
of the trip. Everyone had looked forward to that mo-

ment with more than ordinary interest. It was to be the end of a long journey and the beginning of a week of pleasures and sightseeing. It was no wonder then that when the city was announced, the men thronged the windows and platforms of the cars and gazed curiously at everybody and everything. The quaint old houses interested all, and the thousands of people who thronged the streets were more interesting than the houses. Our reception was more or less of the conventional sort, but there were some things about it that were curious. The people turned out *en masse*, and flocked about the cars with words of kindly greeting.

The train was taken far into the city before the signal to alight was given. It was rather warm, but the boys did not realize it for awhile. The fact, however, that the thermometer stood at 78° in the shade, was more or less impressed on their minds before they reached their quarters. Of course we alighted from the cars in heavy marching order—as we had left New York. That meant overcoats on and the heavy knapsacks capped with blankets. Everybody else was happy and cool in light summer costumes. The military drawn up about the stopping place consisted of the Battalion of Louisiana Field Artillery, Colonel Le Gardeur, commanding; the Veteran Company of the Washington Artillery, Captain C. L. C. Dupuy, commanding; the Battalion of Washington Artillery, Colonel Horton, commanding; the Continental Guards; the Charleston Cadets, and the Boston Lancers.

Then came the Seventy-first in four companies, double rank formation, of course. It was a very curious thing to us to see all the other organizations marching in single rank, and we seemed a genuine curiosity to them because we marched as the tactics provides.

"I see you still preserve the old lock step," said a uniformed gentleman to the writer.

"Why do you call it the old lock step?" was the response.

"Why it is all out of date, is it not?"

This conversation with a military man serves to show how unpopular the double rank formation was supposed to be. Indeed this matter was so seriously considered, that Colonel Vose was requested at one time to march the command in column of fours at single rank distance, but after consultation with the commandants of companies, concluded to preserve the regular formation. This was wise, because it served to distinguish Ours on all parades from every other organization, except the Marines of the North Atlantic Squadron, who marched as we did, of course. The solid appearance the column of companies in double rank gave the battalion, popularized it, until the second or third day we received cheers and congratulations for what had first been looked upon as entirely out of all precedent. When everything was ready, the line of march was taken up, down St. Charles, to Lafayette street, to Camp, to Canal, to St. Charles, to Poydras, to the Levee. The march was a perfect ovation.

The streets were filled with people, who applauded continually, the houses were decorated, while from every window some lady fair waved a welcome. If there ever was a time for the Regiment to do its best it was then. As is often the case, the men felt this so keenly that they marched wretchedly. It was hot enough though for July, and the moisture poured down their faces and trickled cheerfully from the chin-straps. This was some excuse for bad marching. When the Arsenal of the Washington Artillery was reached there was a halt. Amid the clashing of the bands and the cheers of the people, it was more or less difficult to understand what was going on. The Colonel rode up and down the line, the very picture of misery, the end of his sword dripping (not with gore), and the end of his nose glistening like a dew drop of an early morning in May. The Major, with one eye on the open door of the Arsenal, and the other on the battalion, stood (in a position similar to the pose of Ajax defying the lightning) seemingly defying the sun to a fiercer attack. Then Major General Behan rode along the line, his swarthy features smiling and his black eyes flashing response to the sun, which by this time had raised the thermometer to only 80°, though it felt like 180°. Suddenly Jenks was observed to straighten up and twirl his baton. The line was moving! A few steps brought us to the entrance of the Arsenal, and we turned in. Along the lines of the Washington Artillery to the further end of the great hall, larger, if anything, than that of the Seventh, at home, we marched and stood around tables, on which were placed goblets of champagne punch. The delightful coolness of the place lingered with the boys for days, and the delightful fragrance of the punch lingers with them yet. Goblet after goblet was hastily swallowed and there was no unpleasant effect. One could not but exclaim with Pope:

"There shallow draughts intoxicate the brain,
And drinking largely sobers us again.

In the centre of the hall was a great platform, over which was hung the original painting of the meeting of Lee and Jackson, many copies of which are to be found through the Southern country. It was a very cheerful scene altogether. Cheer upon cheer rose from the men in the building to be taken up by the thousands on the outside, until everything shook. A moment between drinks was snatched to listen to addresses of welcome, very short ones, from Colonel Horton, Major General Behan, Mayor Shakespeare, Brigadier General Glinn and Mr. Albert Baldwin, President of the Royal Host, to which Colonel Vose responded of course, and the boys let go of the punch glasses long enough to give the regimental cheer. Then we marched to the Levee, and down to our boat, the Robert E. Lee. In some respects we were fortunate in regard to our quarters, in others most unfortunate. I was just about to say that the fact of our boat being on the river, was a happy thing in its way, but the boat was not on the river. It was on the mud, a portion of it, and the other portion propped up against the Levee.

The fact is, the Robert E. Lee had broken her (more properly his) shaft, and was laid up for repairs. If it had not been for that, the Lord knows what we would have done for quarters, for every house in New Orleans was full. She, or he was lying alongside the planking of the Levee, and an enormous gang plank made a passage to her, or his main deck an easy matter. From her or his main deck, a wide stairway led to the deck above, on which were the cabins and saloons. These cabins and staterooms were very comfortable, but the boat was too far away from the centre of civilization. That was a great disadvantage, it was entirely too far away from the restaurant where the meals were served. That was a greater disadvantage, besides, there were a number of smaller disadvantages. But there were advantages too. Beside us, rolled the great Mississippi, which from its source, amid the jagged rocks and icy towers, thousands of miles away, slowly like, youthful Titan, gathers strength and pursues its majestic course, until it reigns over the valley it blesses. It was worth a journey of two thousand miles to sit on the decks of our steamer and watch the muddy waters of this Empress of streams as they danced and sparkled on their way to the sea. Near us were anchored the North Atlantic Squadron, United States Navy, about us were hundreds of steamboats, large and small, hugh flat bottomed things, lying dormant in the day, and puffing about like monsters in the night. Towards the shore, there was the long line of cotton bales, the thousands of colored flags marking

the owners or consigners of freight, the darkeys working,
pulling here and rolling there, occasionally falling up
against the wrong end of a wise and patient mule, and in
the back ground rose the City, the sun gilding its roofs
and spires. It was a pleasant place to be quartered after
all. The men were assigned bunks in the staterooms, and
some who could not be accommodated in that way, were
given cots in the main saloon. When everybody had been
settled, it was nearly dinner time, and the arrival of Commissary Jacob Hess was anxiously awaited. He came.
He told the boys that they were to be fed at Delmonico's,
whereat, the enthusiasm was intense. There was something about the name, that charmed, even though "Louis"
were a couple of thousand miles away. Each man got a
ticket like this :

DELMONICO RESTAURANT.

Good for one Meal.

— ++ —

SEVENTY-FIRST REGIMENT.

With a ticket in hand, each man started for the restaurant. But alas and alack, they did not stop to inquire
the way, and so

> " Went up the town
> And down the town,
> And round about the middle."

before their eyes were feasted with a sign, reading .

DINING ROOMS
— OF THE —
SEVENTY-FIRST REGIMENT
UP STAIRS.

The dinner was not bad by any means. There was chicken and roast beef, soup, vegetables, relishes, coffee and pies for the first meal, and the average was about the same during the stay.

The Robert E. Lee was an interesting boat. It is one of the largest on the river. The cabins are very much like those of our large boats at home, except that everything is on one deck—that is everything concerning the passengers. Compared to our boats, it is what living in a flat is to living in a seven story and mansard house. Once on board the Lee, and on the saloon deck, no one ever thinks of going down on the lower deck any more than they would think of dropping over a museum tank, and into a cage of anacondas, because this lower deck is given up entirely to cotton and fifty or so deck hands, as wild and turbulent as men can be. No one ever goes down except the officers, and they invariably drag a gatling gun after them. Hardly a trip is completed unaccompanied by a stabbing afray among the deck hands, and in many instances, these affairs end fatally. These men are never allowed above and the saloon boys never go down to the main deck. When they do, they very frequently remain down in a "demition moist" state. This main deck is

the same deck upon which the ladies cabin is situated, on
our boats, and very frequently the dining rooms, retiring
rooms, bars and clerk's and captain's rooms. In some
instances, as on the North river and Sound boats, the
dining-room is situated below this main deck. On the Lee
all this was reversed. There was nothing on the main
deck for a passenger; even his baggage was carried to
the deck above. The place was reserved for the freight,
the roaring fires and fighting crew. There was nothing
below except a very shallow hold, in which a man could
hardly stand upright, for the Lee, like many Mississippi
boats, is flat bottomed and very broad of beam. It is
hardly necessary to say that none but the saloon stewards
remained on board when we took possession. Engineers,
firemen and deck-hands took a holiday. The main deck was
deserted. This deck was opened fore and aft, and the
saloons and cabins looked as if they were only stuck up
on posts, and removable at pleasure. The guard of heavy
timber, running all around the deck, was only about two
feet high. About amidship were the boilers and engines.
The boilers were not enclosed but stood on the deck, open
at both sides to the river, and covered above only by the
saloon flooring. The space between decks was very great.
The engines, there were two of them, were queer looking
things, utterly different from anything seen in our waters.
There was an engineer on each side of the boat. It looked
as if there was an enormous waste of space, but there
wasn't. The Lee ran between New Orleans and Vicksburg,

and her principal carrying trade was cotton. Enormous
quantities of this could be placed on the main deck. It
would fill up the space, tier on tier, until the bales would
rise several feet above even the guard rails of the saloon
deck. At night this lower deck, with its long posts sup-
porting the upper deck, its dark and dingy machinery,
and its deserted look, was a gruesome place. Did you
ever go into a deserted saw mill, near a wood, and an old
mill pond, at night?—a haunted mill? There is something
of that sort in every country district. Well if you did'nt,
try it the first chance you get, and there analyze your
feelings. The writer stood at midnight amid the deep
shadows of the Lee's lower deck, and watched the weird
shapes the flickering light of his lantern cast (there was
some-one with him, you may depend) and saw in fancy the
great fires roaring; heard the clanking of machinery, the
scurrying here and there of the sixty or seventy black
deck hands ; heard the hoarse whistle sound in response
to another, the quick jingle of the bell, to stop ! to back!
to go ahead ! heard the sharp exclamation of the engineer
"we just grazed her !" saw a rush toward two fighting
negroes; heard a dull thud and a cry of anguish, and, as
they carried the body aft, the words "knew that cuss
would get knifed this trip." Then the scene changed,
and in the fitful light, he saw a procession of shades, who
rolled the cotton, laughed and joked, and fought as they
might have done in life, but there was no sound save the
hollow echo of his foot falls as he hurried away to get
a big drink, and go to bed.

CHAPTER VII

SUNDAY NIGHT.

"Why such impress of shipwrights, whose sore task
Does not divide the Sunday from the week?
What might be toward, that this sweaty haste
Doth make the night joint laborer with the day?"
—*Shaks.*

I⊤ was Sunday night and no one seemed to know it, so busy had the hours been and so exciting was the situation. It is perhaps wrong to say no one, for it is claimed by some that Dr. Carlos Martyn, the Chaplain, did remember it, and even went so far as to suggest to one or two of the officers that a regimental service would be a proper

and refreshing thing after so long a journey. Of course
the officers agreed with him, but disappeared very suddenly immediately after. The Chaplain, however, was
not to be humbugged in that fashion. If he could not
have a service of his own, he would attend some one else's.
So he went to church. At least he says he went to church,
and as no one else even made that claim, no one dared
dispute him. Besides all this, the Chaplain's record in
the regiment is good, because there isn't an officer with
whom he has not wrestled at some period, in the hope of
reform. That was an eventful night for the Chaplain, and
not entirely uneventful for many others. What he did
and how he served is best told by himself, in his admirable lecture, delivered at the Thirty-fourth Street Reformed
Church, after the return. The Chaplain says:

"Remembering that it was Sunday night, the Chaplain
resolved to attend church, especially as it had been found
impossible, amid the tumultuous experiences of the day,
to hold a regimental service. Making his way along the
streets, he was pleased to see that the warehouses and
shops were as closely shut as in New York, though he
learned, to his regret, that in the evening the theatres
were always open.

In due season the First Presbyterian Church was
sighted and entered. Though the streets were gay with
uniforms and noisy with revelry, it gratified the Chaplain to find the house of God crowded with worship-
ers—the finest evening congregation he had seen for

many a day, and, as he was told, not exceptional in that church. Having listened to a masterly sermon from the pastor, the Rev. Dr. Palmer, the Chaplain elbowed his way out, intending to return to his quarters.

In this connection it becomes my duty as a truthful historian, to relate a painful story. As the Chaplain, a sedate and sober man, as you know, was walking on with characteristic decorum, and, with a propriety suited to the day, running over in his mind the points of that excellent sermon, he fell—*not from grace*—but he certainly fell. There could be no doubt about that. The fall was too emphatic to permit question. You see, the gutters of New Orleans are peculiar. They are low towards the street and raised towards the sidewalk, and are half as wide as the Mississippi. Their safe navigation demands both knowledge and agility. A stranger from rural New York, the Chaplain was defective in these points. Essaying the passage, he stubbed his toe—and lay sprawling! "My stars!" exclaimed he — nothing stronger, upon honor. That remark he thought appropriate. He *saw* stars. By and bye he picked himself up, collected his scattered fragments and proceeded to take an account of stock, with the following result: Two badly soiled hands; one very dirty coat; one ditto pair of pants, with a huge rent across the left knee, and a shin seriously wounded in this battle of New Orleans—General Jackson! how it ached. What to do? That was the question. Now, the Chaplain is a wise man in his generation. He knew that

if he returned to the boat in that plight it would be difficult to persuade the unregenerate that he had been to
church. Appearances were certainly against him. In a
dazed and uncertain way he limped towards the St.
Charles Hotel, hugging the shadows, hailed a cab, and
without stopping to higgle over the fare, had himself
driven to the neighborhood of the boat. Alighting on
the levee, he paid the cabman, Then the long military
cloak he wore was artistically adjusted. Hanging it over
those two dirty hands, lifting it well up, so that it should
cover the soiled coat, and letting it trail to his boots in
a way that hid the damaged trowsers and the outrageous
rent in the knee, the Chaplain threw back his head,
rushed past the guard at the gangway, glared defiantly
at the men scattered through the saloon, as who should
say :

> "Thou canst not say I did it ; never shake
> Thy gory locks at me. "

opened his state-room door, and vanished.

But the story leaked out. The Chaplain was the victim
of misplaced confidence. In a moment of weakness, but
with the charming frankness characteristic of an innocent
nature, he embosomed himself to the surgeon of the regiment, expecting sympathy—and silence. He remembered that it is the function of a physician to believe im-
probable stories. Well, he got the sympathy, but the silence?—no ! The next day, at a private dinner party, the
irreverent doctor gave his version of the adventure—a

version, I am bound to acknowledge, highly complimentary to his inventive genius. Thereafter the Chaplain was kept busy until bed time making explanations—just as though he had been a Congressman !

While the Chaplain was at church, or wrestling with the knotty points of Dr. Palmer's sermon in the quiet of the cabin of the Lee, his comrades were scattered about the city, in quest of adventure. By nine o'clock none remained on board but the guard, and they were only there in flesh. Their spirits were in the city. Everything was new and strange. The weather was simply perfect. The moon rose over the city and seemed to hover there, while the evening star gleamed close beside it. It was a perfect crescent, and the conjunction appeared to augur that the stars thought well of the crescent city below—so brilliant and gay. As the Chaplain has sorrowfully remarked, the theatres were all open, and the audiences were large too. In some of them uniforms—blue uniforms—could have been seen. The city was very gay indeed. The principal streets were filled with merry people, who laughed and chatted good humoredly. It was a very different crowd than that of our streets on Sunday night. The church goers and theatre goers mingled harmoniously, each giving the other credit for knowing what pleased them. All about one heard the rattle of foreign languages; French, which is almost as common as English, Spanish, Italian and German, with all the variations those languages are susceptible of.

As a matter of fact New Orleans is two cities in one, with Canal street for a dividing line. On either side are to be found the French and Spanish and the American town, but the social lines are not as carefully drawn as the geographical. Canal street is an avenue of great beauty, two hundred feet wide, with sidewalks and carriage ways on each side, and in the centre a raised space, planted with two rows of trees, called the "neutral ground" and utilized by a line of street cars. The French or Spanish town is very interesting in its antique quaintness. The streets are very narrow, and diverge in an irregular and abrupt way. A walk through them recalled similar strolls in France and Spain, and the occasional sound of voices singing and conversing in those languages adds to the illusion. It may be, doubtless it is, a morbid feeling which prompts the meditative man to pause and look up at the stones of some old house, thinking the while how long those inanimate blocks will remain there, and how many others will gaze up at them when the present beholder is mouldering into dust. Such thoughts may be morbid, but the old Spanish town of New Orleans engendered them on that moonlit Sunday night. With that came another thought, that, could the kindred thoughts of others have been impressed on those old stones, how they would be covered with inscriptions. The stones are there. Their builders are gone, yet nature is as gay, the moon shines as bright, men are as busy in gain-getting as in the years that are past. Well may we exclaim :

Who peopled all the city streets
A hundred years ago ?
Who filled the church with faces meek
A hundred years ago?
The sneering tale
Of sister frail,
The plot that work'd
A brother's hurt ;
Where, O ! where are the plots and sneers,
The poor man's hopes, the rich man's fears,
Of a hundred years ago?

Whether the men spent the evening in contemplation of the houses or otherwise the writer knows not, though he inclines somewhat toward the latter idea, but certain it is that the ponderous doors of the guard house yawned rather often after midnight, to engulf the luckless wight who had overstaid his pass.   It was long after the "witching hour " when the lonely sentry could accurately count the snores of his comrades, who were dreaming of the morning that was to usher in the King.

CHAPTER VIII.

He's a king,
A true, right king, that dares do aught save wrong;
Fears nothing mortal, but to be unjust;
Who is not blown up with the flatt'ring puffs
Of spongy sycophants; who stands unmoved
Despite the justling of opinion.
                                        —*Marston.*

ON Monday afternoon His Majesty, Rex, came. His approach had been heralded for days with as much care as though he bore the mightiest sceptre in the universe. Every morning the papers published double leaded and double headed bulletins of the King's condition and his whereabouts. His arrival at the Jetties was flaunted in the face of every man, woman and child who read a New Orleans paper. There were columns of proclamations and edicts. The clerks of the "department of state" were

busy for days under the direction of Warwick, Earl Marshal, and Bathurst, Lord High Chamberlain of the Empire,
completing the final details for his reception and working up the public sentiment to a just appreciation of the
honor that was about to be conferred on the city. While
all this hubbub was in progress the Royal Host and the
Societies connected with it were quietly preparing for the
processions of Tuesday. No one seemed to know just
where these preparations were being made or by whom
they were directed. No one seemed to care. Everyone
knew that there was to be a scenic display that was promised to far eclipse anything of the kind they had ever seen.
Where it was to come from troubled no one. They were
satisfied that the arrangements were in proper hands and
that in good time they would see all that was promised.
The chariots and floats would have made Barnum sick
with envy, but the places where they were stored put to
blush the dreariness of circus tents off duty. There was
no crowd about the place though ; no women and children
pushed and struggled to get a glimpse through the half
open doors and no small boys climbed, at the risk of their
necks, the peaks and gables of the adjoining houses.
Had such a mass of scenic treasure been stored in New
York it would have taken half a thousand policemen to
keep the place from being overrun.

A large steamboat went down the river, starting early
in the morning. There was gathered on board a select
company of ladies and gentlemen. The boat went down

the river "to meet the King," but just where His Majesty
got on board was kept a profound mystery.   When about
five miles away from the city, it was announced that His
Majesty was in the grand saloon and, amid the popping of
champagne corks, his health was drank and his praises
sung.

"The presence of a king engenders love
Among his subjects, and his royal friends."

The steamer stood up the river towards Canal street
and presently the levee, black with his surging subjects,
came in view.   It was a sight long to be remembered.
Along the river front, flanked with hundreds of bales of
cotton, stood thousands of men, women and children
awaiting his coming.   Away up Canal street, royal itself
in appearance, as far as the eye could reach were, line
upon line, the glittering bayonets and waving plumes of
the military.   Close upon the river's front were the blue
uniforms of Ours and the United States Marines.   A hundred gallant horsemen,—Dukes of the Empire every one
—gay in the royal purple and gold, awaited their master's
coming at the landing stage.   There was a salvo of artillery as his Majesty stepped on the sacred soil of his capital city.   Never did monarch enter a gayer capital.   Since
the royal fleet had set sail from Utopia nature had smiled
upon his favorite.   The clouds had fled from the heavens,
the soft breezes had come up from the tropics and stayed
long enough to burst the buds, open the sweet violets and
raise the grass above the sod.   He landed amid the cheers

of thousands, the waving of flags and the booming of cannon. Batteries roared on the shore and the heavy ordnance of the North Atlantic squadron, United States Navy,
shook the houses. No monarch ever entered a more loyal
city. As his boat came up the river, covered with craft
crowded with the beauty of New Orleans, the yards of the
men-of-war were manned, the ships dressed and the highest honors paid him. More could not have been done
had Rex been monarch from Pole to Pole. Amid the
plaudits of the people he mounted the royal carriage and
passed through long lines of military gathered to do him
honor. About half way up the line there came a pause:

> "The guards mechanically formed in ranks
> Playing, at beat of drum, their martial pranks;
> Shouldering and standing as if struck to stone,
> While condescending Majesty looks on."

The Mayor on bended knee presented the golden keys
of the city resting on cushions of purple velvet. Drums
rolled, cannons roared, swords flashed in air, standards
drooped and Rex was King indeed.

Then came the military parade escorting the King to
the Opera House. The post of honor was accorded to
Ours and the colonel commanded the first division of the
Imperial army, which consisted of the marines, regulars,
Seventy-first, three regiments of Louisiana troops and two
batteries of artillery. The two other divisions were equally
imposing. Amid the pomp and ceremony of the arrival
proclamations were distributed broadcast, calling on the
people to make merry on the morrow with decorum and
propriety.

There can be no question of the seriousness of the New Orleans Carnival. It costs a great deal of money and a great deal of time, which, by the way, is not regarded as so exact an equivalent for money in the South as we in New York regard it. This marching and counter marching, this blaring of trumpets and issuing of proclamations means something. It is a huge business speculation, sustained by the leaders of trade, fostered by the wealth and fashion of the city and invariably successful. There is nothing of the cheap tinsel or advertising humbug about it. Even the reception of the King, exquisitely rediculous as it may appear to the calmer reflection, is not devoid of reason. The King is an ideal monarch. He represents in his royal person, whoever he may be, the beau ideal of chivalry and good fellowship. The entire city gives itself up to the intoxication of the hour. All business is practically suspended and all classes join in the general joyousness. The organizations that control the Mardi Gras festivities are composed of the leading gentlemen of Louisiana. They give their influence and money towards it and their example is followed by every citizen, however humble his rank or short his purse strings. The city is given up to Momus and his crew, and the poorest has one day of the year to which he can look forward as bringing a rest from labors and a succession of pageants that cost him nothing. Thousands of strangers come to New Orleans and the country merchants take the occasion for their annual buying trip. The thousands of dollars spent by the Royal Host and kindred societies are returned to the merchants by the thousands who throng the streets for days before.

Early in the morning almost before the sun has gilded the muddy Mississippi the streets are filled with a good natured, chaffing, hustling crowd. Men, women and children in masks and dominos walk about in the utmost good fellowship.

> " City, country, all
> Is in gay triumph tempest toss'd,
> I scarce could press along. The trumpet voice
> Is lost in loud repeated shouts."

It might be suggested that the entire freedom that is indulged in would lead to excesses. Such, however, is not the case. The writer took especial pains to inquire as to the police returns for the day and he was assured that the percentage of arrests was very slightly increased if at all. He did not see one grossly intoxicated person in the streets.

The processions were all that was claimed for them. With the arrival of the King came a parade that discount- ed our old time Fourth of July parades at home. Up one street and down another, under a very indulgent sun, they marched. But there was some satisfaction in the matter, for cheers and praises were showered on them. The bat- talion did do well. The men had got over their nervous- ness and, with white trousers, looked and marched better than they had in many a day. The Colonel commanded the brigade, including the regulars, and Major McAlpin

did the honors for the battalion in a very handsome manner. Captain J. R. Denman distinguished himself by
riding a blooded mare up and down the brigade line, carrying orders for General Vose, until horse and rider
smoked. The Captain was a member of the staff of
Brigadier General Plume, of New Jersey, and was one of
the guests of the regiment and a volunteer on the General's staff. He rode well and furiously, and naturally enough
came to grief, the mare slipping on the smooth pavements
and falling prone. In a moment, however, both were up
and Denman at it again, much to the dissatisfaction of a
number of surgeons who were hastening from all quarters.
Fortunate Denman !

In the procession of Tuesday the battalion took no
part whatever and the men were given seats where they
could best view the pageants. The band was chosen as
the "Court band," which immediately preceded His
Majesty and divided the honors with him. The processions were two in number. One took place in the day—
all day it seemed to be moving—and was certainly a magnificent affair. The wagons and floats bearing the tableaux
were most beautiful and there was nothing in any of them
that suggested an advertisement or an immodest thought.
When it is said that the very best people not only encour-
age these carnival processions, but *take part in them*, their
wonderful success may be the more readily understood.
The streets were filled with thousands of maskers, the
windows and balconies gay with sightseers and everybody

smiling and cheerful. No one could spend Mardi Gras in New Orleans without believing in the genuiness of the happy disposition of the people. The theme of the day procession was the Arabian Night's Tales and was illustrated by tableaux prepared carefully and at great expense. The costumes were new and pretty and the interpreters intelligent. First came the Herald, then a detachment of police, the court band, Earl Marshal Guards, Grand Vizier, standard bearers, Hindoo priests and the bœuf gras. Then came twenty-three cars containing tableaux in the order named, the prominent figures in the groups being richly attired and the attendants appropriately costumed. The first car contained King Schahriar seated on his throne, followed by the court officers and attendants. The other cars contained the Princess Scheherazade ; Third Voyage of Sinbad ; Fifth Voyage of Sinbad ; Story of Zobeide ; Story of Beker and Gishara ; King of the Black Isles : Three Calendars ; Second Royal Mendicant ; Third Royal Mendicant ; Story of the Third Calendar ; Barber and His Seven Brothers ; History of Prince Zeyn Alasham ; Nine Diamond Statues ; Forty Thieves; Baba Abdallah ; Enchanted House ; Aladdin in the Cave ; Aladdin's Banquet : Abou Hassan; Prince Ahmed and the Lions; Little Hunchback; Story of the Envious Man. Then followed comical displays of the Independent Order of the Moon and the Phunny Phorty Phellows and promiscuous maskers on foot and in the vans.

The evening procession was perhaps more magnificent

than that of the day, probably because of the wonderful effect of the well managed lights.   It was under the auspices of the "Mistick Krewe of Comus" and had for a theme the Myths of the Northland.   The story of Sigurd, the Valsung and the fall of the Niblung was magnificently told in pictures of living fire.   First came Comus and his " Krewe " attired in blue and silver and following were seventeen tableaux in the order named : The Genius of the Northland; Gods of Scandinavia; The sword in the Branstock; Death of Sigmund; House of Reidmar; The Treasures of the World; At the Waterfall; The Workshop of the Dwarfs; Elfland, The Bower of Gudrun; Grunhield Preparing the Magic Drink; The Voyage of the Niblungs; The Last of the Niblungs; The Hell of the Northland; Valhalla; Ragnarok; The Twilight of the Gods.

CHAPTER IX.

DINING WITH THE GOVERNOR.

> 'Tis the middle watch of a summer's night,
> The earth is dark, but the heavens are bright;
> Naught is seen in the vault on high
> But the moon, and the stars and the cloudless sky.
> —*Drake.*

> I cry you halt, my master;
> You pass not here save at the word
> Of command.
> —*Anon.*

THE days went rapidly enough in New Orleans. One pleasure succeeded another so rapidly that it was not until after the return home that the men fully appreciated the great courtesy with which they had been treated. It was one grand hurly burly of delights—no sooner out of one than in another. The programme was varied. It is quite impossible to begin to give a list of the private courtesies shown individuals. The battalion arrived on Sunday morning. On that evening the theatres were opened to them, private houses were open to them, nothing was closed to them, except the boat where the battalion was quartered, and that only to those who got in after midnight and had to make peace with the officer of the guard. In connection with that idea the following bit of conversation between a belated private and the officer of the guard is interesting.

Officer : " Why did you overstay your pass? "

Private : " Couldn't help it."

Officer : " Have to try the guard house with you then !"

Private : " That's pretty rough ! "

Officer : (Sharply) " What's pretty rough ? "

Private : " Well now look here, Lieutenant. I come down here to New Orleans as a guest of the city. Received by the Mayor and City council. Citizens treat me kindly. Influential citizen—State Senator or assistant Govenor or rich planter or something like that—invites me to his house the first pop. I go. Am introduced to his charming family. Behaved beautifully. Did the regiment credit. Asked to come again. Start for home. Got there a little late. Forget all about the pass. Corporal of the guard grabs me. You lock me up. Dine with the Govenor and get locked up because I'm too polite to leave before the proper time. That's what I call pretty rough ? "

If the men did not dine with the Govenor every day, they were just as kindly treated and probably had just as good dinners. On Monday the King came, and the magnificence of that event and the battalion's part in it is told in another chapter. The same afternoon the Royal Host presented the now famous banner. Tuesday was spent in viewing the Mardi Gras processions and the great balls of the evening. On Wednesday the battalion had a dress parade. On Thursday morning the graves of the Confederate soldiers were saluted and on the same afternoon the Battalion had a most succesful reception on board the Robert E. Lee. On Friday morning the train was boarded and the homeward journey begun. It can readily be seen by this programme that the time of the men was fully occupied. The pass system for the men was abandoned after the first night and afterwards they went and came pretty much as they pleased except that they were on hand for drills and parades. A number of very amusing incidents are related of the first night. One has already been told.

It was about four o'clock in the morning—four hours after midnight—that the sentry at the gangway heard the sound of stealthy footsteps. He had been warned to look out for petty theives who might possibly smuggle themselves on board and despoil the sleeping "Yanks," so he remained very quietly in the shade of a post and watched intently the movements of the mysterious figure on the levee. The figure paused behind a cotton bale and

A RECONNOITRE.

peered cautiously around the corner. The sentry saw him dimly outlined in the flickering light of the gangway lantern, but he did not see the sentry. This evidently assured him that the coast was clear, that the sentinels had been withdrawn for some reason, and he boldly started for the gangway. When just about to step on the plank, it occured to him that something was wrong. There was an unnatural quiet about the deck, so he retreated to the cotton bale again. The sentry stole through the shadows and brought the nodding corporal of the guard to his feet with a fierce hiss-ss-s ! The man behind the cotton bale heard the click of the corporal's rifle and sank down behind the bale and out of sight. A few words of explanation to the corporal aroused that officer's interest, and he in turn aroused the Sergeant of the guard. Two or three men were placed about the deck at favorite points, and the Sergeant took a seat on a camp chest mentally resolving to capture the bold marauder or perish at his post. Silence had reigned for about twenty minutes when the figure crept quietly out from behind the cotten bale and started towards the bow of the boat evidently intending to climb up the sides. He slipped as he made the attempt and rolled down on the levee. Then he got up and evidently intending to end the matter, made straight for the gangway and on tip toe passed to the main deck. With a half suppressed chuckle at his success he was just about ascending the stairway when he was seized by four men who came out of the gloom, and in a moment was on his back, struggle as he might. A large piece of dark paper muslin enveloped his head and body. It was the work of a moment to unwind this and disclose the uniform of the regiment and a well known face.

"Well I'm d—d" said the Sergeant, supremely disgusted.

"So am I" meekly answered the prisoner, who by this time had recovered his breath.

"Where is your pass?"

"Haven't got any."

"Good night and pleasant dreams" added the Sergeant, as the door closed on the luckless private.

It was only about twenty minutes after this that the same sentry heard a quick step approaching the gangway. A private hurried up much out of breath. There was no pause this time.

"Halt there" was the order.

"Oh don't stop me. I have a very important message for the officer of the day and must deliver it at once."

"You can wait a moment I think, until I call the Sergeant. Please do," said the sentry, bringing his bayonet down to within an inch and a quarter of the soldier's buttons. The Sergeant came and was so impressed with the man's earnestness that he took him to the Lieutenant of the Guard. The latter sent him to the cabin of the officer of the day, who had just turned in.

"What do you want" roared that official from the inside.

"There is a man here sir, who says he has a message for you—an important message."

" Who is it from ? "

" He says from the Mayor, sir."

Of course the officer arose and opened the door, think-ing what on earth the Mayor of New Orleans meant by sending a message at that time of night. With a salute the Sergeant explained the matter and the prisoner hand-ed a note. It read as follows :

ST. CHARLES HOTEL.
Sunday Night.

To the Officer of the Day,
Seventy-first Regiment.

Please excuse Private ——, of your Regiment, for overstaying his pass. He was with me all evening and I have detained him against his will to assist me in arranging some details of to-morrow's procession.

Yours truly,
JAMES SHAKESPEARE,
Mayor of New Orleans.

Unfortunately for the messenger, the officer of the day happened to know that, in the first place, the Mayor had nothing to do with arranging the procession, and in the second place, that His Honor's name was Joseph and not James. So the doors of the dungeon opened again and the much humbugged Sergeant took great pleasure in personally attending to the opening. The man was known afterwards as the " Assistant Mayor."

While the guard house is under consideration there might as well be related another incident. The officers of the battalion took with them to New Orleans several colored servants. Commissary Hess had one named Jep, who worked in the Commissary's car while on the road and waited on that officer when in the city. Jep was a great, strapping fellow, good natured and obliging. It was on Wednesday evening that he permitted himself to become more or less hilarious. About nine o'clock he came on board and went directly to his master's cabin where, of course, he had access at all times. After staying in there for some time he went out on the upper deck and watched the twinkling lights of the city. Then he thought of the dusky belles whose eyes twinkled just as brightly. Sinking into a chair he dreamed that, instead of being what he was, he suddenly became transformed into an officer. On his shoulders were the heavy epaulets, at his side the shining sword and from his shako nodded the white plumes of authority. He saw himself among the colored girls—the lion of the evening, petted and feasted and admired above all his comrades. He awoke with a start to find himself chilly in the night air and the same old Jep with the same private's uniform on his back. His dream affected him and, as he went slowly into the cabin, he formed an idea. Of course it took Jep some time to form an idea in its entirety, but with hard work and deter- mination he succeeded. He went into Commissary Hess's· cabin and taking out that officer's uniform, laid it on the bed. On the breast of the coat sparkled the decoration of the King, the gold and buttons seemed brighter to Jep than they ever had before. Why could he not be an offi- cer? There were the materials of which officers were made. He had nothing to do but make himself into one,

AMBITIOUS "JEP."

slip past the sentinels and cry havoc with the hearts of the
girls who would recognize at once that he was now in his
proper sphere. Laboriously Jep put on the uniform,
girded on the sword and looked out. The saloon was deserted save by a few who nodded. Away he went, down
the length of the room, past the dozing corporal of the
guard and out on the deck. As he turned to go down, his
arm struck a projecting piece of wood work and the rattle
of the sword attracted the attention of the sentry on the
stairs who stood "at attention" as the "officer" went by. Jep
turned his head and the whites of his eyes gleamed on the
startled soldier who, knowing that the Govenor had been
figuratively raising the deuce with other regiments, in-
stantly surmised that he had raised his satanic majesty in
proper person and commisisoned him in the Seventy-first !
The alarm was given and Jep was secured—not without
a struggle however—the uniform stripped from him and
he safely stowed in the lockup. There he sat—his hopes
blasted, his spirits crushed—head in hands, with the tears
insinuating themselves between his fingers, a picture of
misery. When Commissary Hess came on board the case
was presented to him, and, with his great good nature, he
urged Jep's release and forgiveness.

CHAPTER X.

ACROSS THE CHASM.

"By the flow of the inland river
  Whence the fleets of iron have fled,
  Where the blades of green grass quiver,
  Asleep are the ranks of the dead;
      Under the soil and the dew
      Waiting the judgement day,
      Love and tears for the blue,
      Tears and love for the gray."
                                    —*Finch.*

No one seemed to know just who suggested the idea of a salute to the Confederate dead. It was an inspiration born of a desire to do something in return for the kindnesses heaped upon the party by the living soldiers of the South. The Battalion could do nothing for them, but it could honor their dead with a soldier's salute. It was in harmony, too, with the course of the Seventy-first. Among the first at the initial battle of twenty years ago and the last to leave the field, where its dead were lying beside those of Louisiana regiments, it was the first to give a soldier's greeting to the soldier dead. When it was announced to the command that they were to march to Greenwood Cemetery and fire a salute, the men were anxious to start at once. There was a unanimous approval of the idea. They felt that it was not an expedition ordered by the officers and obeyed by the men because they were soldiers. It was an expedition in which every man felt a personal interest—a genuine satisfaction. A firing party of fifty were ordered to prepare. Major E. A. McAlpin and two Captains commanded, while the Colonel, other line officers and the staff accompanied the detachment as lookers on. The New Orleans City Railroad had placed a number of cars drawn by a dummy at the Battalion's disposal and the men were taken to the cemetery gates.* Greenwood is a peculiar looking cemetery at first glance. The graves are all raised above ground and are really tombs. This is necessary on account of the nature of the soil. Dig down anywhere for three or four feet and water is found. Obviously, then, the dead must be placed above ground, not in it. The gateway and approaches to the cemetery were crowded with ladies and gentlemen. The line was formed and, with the band playing a funeral march, at reverse arms the men went slowly in and around the Confederate monument. A halt was ordered and the

*Appendix B.

rifles loaded. Amid an impressive silence the officers uncovered, the people crowded about, and Dr. Martyn, the chaplain, stepped forward.

"Stoop angels, hither from the skies !
There is no holier spot of ground
Than where defeated valor lies,
By honoring brothers crowned."

Dr. Martyn spoke : "A famous German theologian once said : ' Thank God for sin !' Not that there is anything in sin to be thankful for, but it is the occasion for a display of the divine character impossible without it because unnecessary. Thank God for the war ! War is an unmixed evil. But God is bringing out of it a better mutual understanding and a truer brotherhood. Twenty years ago the North and South fatally misunderstood each other. The North pictured the South as *Bombastes Furioso.* The South looked at the North as a Connecticut peddler. The North believed the South wouldn't fight. The South thought the North couldn't. The battle flags were unfurled. The swords were rough ground. The guns were loaded. The thunder of cannon shook the continent. The world stood aghast. The old misconception disappeared in the smoke of a hundred battle fields. It was mutually discovered that the spirit of '76, of Sumpter and Marion, of Schuyler and Greene, animated their descendants. The hostile sections were awed into a wholesome respect for each others' heroism and self-sacrifice. The old Romans placed the gods of the various principalities incorporated in the empire in their Pantheon—each had his niche. In the Pantheon of American patriotism and honor time shall set Grant and Lee, Jackson and Sherman ; while the shadowy host, heroic as the English Sidney, chivalric as the French Bayard, who poured out life, on the one side for the National idea, on the other for the 'Lost Cause,' open their lips of dust to sing the angelic overture : Glory to God in the highest, on earth peace, good will towards men. As a foretoken of that coming day, nay, as a help towards its inauguration, we salute these graves. Over the chasm filled with blood, filled with tears, filled with bitter, burning memories, we extend the hand of national fraternity, and lock palms with our brothers of the South in eternal friendship."

Major McAlpin's voice was low and solemn as the commands "ready ! aim ! fire !" issued from his lips. Three times the guns rang out and the smoke curled about the monument. The birds twittered wildly and flew in great circles overhead. It was a small tribute, but the shades of the departed seemed to smile proudly down through the smoke on the boys in blue. Many eyes were moistened as the Battalion marched to the cars again through lines of men and women who silently bowed their heads. Verily there was

"Love and tears for the blue,
Tears and love for the gray."

There was another scene while the Battalion was in the Crescent City that, while of a far different nature, was equally impressive. It occured at the Grand Opera House

on the day of the arrival of the King. The salute to the
dead was a tribute of the North to the South ; the ceremonies at the Opera House were a tribute from the South
to the North. It was after the parade on that Monday,
already described, that the Battalion was marched in a
body to the doors of the great theatre. About them stood
members of the Royal Host in full evening dress, the in-
signia of their office glistening on their breasts. It would
be useless to give any of their names. They were the
leading men of the South, while here and there were seen
officers of the Navy and other officials of the United States
Government. The body of the house was crowded with
the fairest women and most notable men. On the stage
were grouped, Govenors, legislators judges, lawyers,
clergymen, bankers, merchants, officers of the United
States Army and Navy—in fact the representative men
of every walk of life. On a throne in the rear sat the
Carnival King, while about him were grouped the Dukes
of the Royal Host. The Battalion was marched in and
occupied the first balcony. The remainder of the house
was packed with ladies and gentlemen. It was a peculiar
scene. Certainly nothing has been seen like it since the
war. On the stage were ex-generals and officials of the
Confederacy mingling with ex-officers of the Federal army
and officers of the active army and navy. Side by side
stood the brother of Admiral Semmes, of the Alabama,
with the Commander of the U. S. S. Kearsage. Was it
possible that these men forgot that the Kearsage had sunk

the Alabama but a few years ago ? Was it possible that
the thunder of the Kearsage's guns in welcoming the King
—the same tone that rang in Semme's ears as his well-
fought Alabama sank beneath him—did not recall the
memories of the past ? Perhaps they had forgotten it :
surely they had forgiven it, for in every action that day—
in every word—those men and women gathered to do
honor to a Northern regiment--breathed but one hope :
that the past might be hidden by the weal of the present
and the golden promises of the future.

Duke Albertus, of Massasoit, (Mr. Albert Baldwin) addressing the King, spoke as follows :

Most Potent Monarch ! with feelings of unalloyed love
and veneration we greet your presence once more in this
your chosen Capital. You have heard at your landing
the roar of our friendly artilery, along the thoroughfares
through which you have passed the glad hazzas of a delighted people, and you see gathered around you the wise
men and fair daughters of our city—representations of
her wisdom, her wealth, her chivalry and her beauty, all
demonstrations of the earnestness with which our hearts
go out to you and the faith which we plight to your house.

Here, too, are the gallant soldiers from a distant quarter
of your realm come to assist us in your welcome and to
add to the glory and renown of your reign. Few gov-
ernments that have ever existed in this world can claim
the same willing obedience, the active co-operation and
a like wild, enthusiastic love as greets Your Majesty at

every step of your triumphant progress. Your's is the province to cheer; your's a mission of pleasure ; your's the power to lighten the burdens of every day life and banish sorrow and care from the heart. No wonder then, that your people join with one accord in demonstrations of joy at your presence in their midst. May it ever be thus, and, as the years roll away, when you annually return to celebrate with us your cherished fete day, may the pageants in your honor each eclipse its predecessor in elegance and beauty.

On behalf of the King, "Bathurst, Lord High Chamberlain," (Hon. George H. Braughn,) responded with rare eloquence, saying in the course of his address : We congratulate you upon the peace and quiet that reigns within your borders ; that, strife and turmoil having entirely ceased, you are indeed a free and happy people. We congratulate you upon the presence of the magnificent military command that has come from the distant North to shake hands in peace with their comrades in arms in the far South, thereby binding and riveting together the feelings and the interests of distant, but yet closely allied sister States. We regard the vistation of these Northern soldiers as the brightest and strongest omen that peace reigns indeed throughout this land and that the Union of the great American States will now be eternal !

The Duke of Chesapeake (Thomas J. Semmes,) then came forward 'bearing the banner'* and spoke as follows :

Soldiers of the Seventy-first Regiment: In obedience

*Appendix C.

to the command of my most puissant King, I am here
to declare his pleasure. Appreciating the fact that
you have come from the distant Northern metropolis
to unite with thousands in doing him honor and acknow-
ledging his sovereignty, my King has been pleased, as a
mark of special favor and esteem, to present to you his
royal colors—the imperial purple, the cloth of gold, the
unfading green—emblematic of his rank, his power and
his everlasting reign. This spectacle has no equal in the
annals of America; indeed, no troops have been thus
honored by my august master. You, soldiers of the
Seventy-first Regiment, receive this standard from a king
whose illustrious descent can be traced through a long
line of ancestors until it reaches the Tarquinian kings
and there fades away in the dim twilight of the Roman
Saturnalia. The reign of this King has not been inter-
rupted by the rise or fall of nations, empires or peoples.
Wars, revolutions, intestine conflicts have unseated the
deified Cæsars, dethroned the descendants of Charlemagne,
discrowned kings and emperors and overturned republics ;
but the sway of the King of the Carnival over his happy
subjects has received no check, for his reign is based on
the ceaseless aspirations of the human heart for human
love and human happiness. The King of the Carnival is
the king of humanity. This banner, therefore, is given
you as a souvenir exclusively devoted to pleasure ; it is no
battle flag ; its use is to be confined to the promotion of
the happiness of man ; it is not destined to the tatters of

victory or of glory ; it is not to be stained with the blood of men or the tears of women and children ; it is emblematic of peace and good will, and, therefore, it is to be unfurled only to receive the pure, gentle, peaceful, perfumed breezes like those which in Paradise

" O'er the four rivers the first waters blew."

That this flag will ever be devoted to peaceful uses is evinced by the interchange of hospitalities between those heretofore engaged in deadly conflict ; by the reverence expressed for the illustrious dead, and the respect paid the distinguished living, regardless of political opinions ; by the national yearning for more intimate intercourse, which the great city of New York is so actively engaged in satisfying ; by the unexpected display of resources and wealth producing energy in the Southern States attested by the census reports and by the marvelous manifestation of the happy condition of the colored people of the South, which their extraordinary increase proclaims in terms not to be contradicted.

Long ago the steel rail connecting North and South has ceased to be a military road for the transportation of troops and the telegraphic wire to be the organ for the transmission of hostile commands ; the rail is to us now only a ribbon of steel, along which flows the electric current of friendship for those who, we believe, we have learned to know and esteem.

Bear, then, this banner home and tell your people that it is the emblem of peace and good will, and with it the

King of the Carnival has sent his royal command that
hereafter all the citizens of this great nation shall be
united and constitute one family, bound together by the
indissoluble ties of friendship and patriotism

Adjutant Frank H. Jordan went forward and took the
staff. It was a trying moment for Colonel Vose—trying
because it was unexpected. Every eye in the vast audience was turned towards him and there was an intense
quiet. His position was more than ordinarily responsible. The least word wrongly applied might have marred
a ceremony that up to this time was in perfect harmony.
It was evident that the emotion of the audience had been
gradually welling up during the eloquent addresses that
had been given. It was the Colonel's opportunity to cap
the climax and none felt the responsibility more than
himself. Many of his own officers, in keen appreciation
of the affair, moved uneasily, but the Colonel rose to
the gravity of the situation. From the moment he com-
menced speaking there was a profound hush, broken
now and again towards the close by a sob. When he
had ceased the applause took the form of a subdued mur-
mer that gradually gathered in force until the very chan-
deliers jingled and the standards trembled with the rush
of cheers. It was more than a pity that some one did not
put in writing the words of that address. He said in
substance that the Seventy-first had little expected
such honors thrust upon it. They had come to New Orleans to grasp the hand of friendship, nothing more.

They had undertaken a long and fatiguing journey, to visit the beautiful city. It was not a small undertaking to bring so many men so long a distance and they did not come for the sake of the hospitalities that were to be shown them, but to tell their brothers of the South how much they esteemed them and loved them, how they had never ceased to esteem them, how, even when duty called them to array themselves in the field, they went forward to the task in fear and trembling to shed a brother's blood and with saddened hearts. But thank God! the dead past is forgotten in the joy of the present, and when in the future there was fighting to be done, they would be found shoulder to shoulder with the soldiers of the South—brothers in fact as in theory. He accepted the beautiful emblem from His Majesty for the Seventy-first and it should be sacredly preserved as a memento of the visit and of the honor conferred upon the regiment. It would surprise the people in the North to learn of the magnificent reception their representative soldiers were having in the far South and their hearts would go out towards those of their Southern brothers in recognition. They would regard the banner as a proclamation from the King of the Carnival commanding that henceforth peace should reign throughout the great land.

CHAPTER XI.

And the night shall be filled with music,
And the cares that infest the day
Shall fold their tents like the Arabs
And as silently steal away.
                                    —*Longfellow.*

THE Mardi Gras balls were numerous and magnificent. Invitations were sent to all of the officers and men and in many instances they were notified that the uniform was the only requirement for admission. It is safe to say that every man of the Battalion attended at least one ball on Tuesday night. The ball of the King was held in the Carnival Palace, an enormous permanent building. The ball-rooms, there are several, are so arranged that they may be all practically thrown into one. This was necessary, for it is said that there were fully twenty thou-

sand ladies and gentlemen present during the evening.
The crush was terrible at first, but after an hour or so the
merry dancers had learned to jostle each other with becoming propriety and good nature. When the King arrived, accompanied by the Queen, (who, by the way, was
the representative of one of the most distinguished fam-
ilies of Louisiana) a passage was cleared and the royal
party, followed by a brilliant staff, after passing around
the ball rooms, retired to an elegant audience chamber
where favored subjects were presented to their Majesties
and drank champagne provided from His Majesty's privy
purse. There were three or four bands of music at the
ball—the principal being that of the Seventy-first—Joyce
and his forty merry fellows. There were no masks worn
at the King's ball, but the costumes were varied and the
scene a wonderfully brilliant one. There joy was un-
confined—

> "No sleep till morn when youth and pleasure meet,
> To chase the glowing hours with flying feet."

There was another ball that night that, amid all the
scenes of beauty and revelry, was supreme. It was that
of the "Misticke Crewe." For years this has been the
annual gathering of the *creme de la creme* of the South.
It compares with our Charity Ball at home in the care
with which invitations are given, in the selectness of its per-
sonality. It exceeds it in the beauty of its arrangement
and in the congregation of fair women, for it has more
than a local reputation and the beauties of many States

are added to its rosebud garden of girls. The French Opera House is something like our Academy, both in size and general appearance. The dancing floor is similarly prepared, while the arrangement of boxes and first balcony is almost exactly like that of the Academy. The public is excluded from the dancing floor at first and the Misticke Krewe, in extraordinary costumes, go through a performance of their own. During this time no gentlemen are permitted to enter the boxes or occupy a seat on the first balcony. Every seat is occupied by a lady. The result is a scene of marvelous beauty. The music of the orchestra is hushed into softness by the fluttering of countless fans and the nodding of plumes on stately heads. The balcony is a bower of flowers clad in the beauty of a thousand stars. At a signal the spell is broken, the great host mingles in the dance and it is many hours before the Lord of Comus gives

"To all, to each a fair good-night,
And pleasant dreams and slumbers light."

On Thursday morning a card was issued to the ladies of New Orleans inviting them to a promenade concert on board the Lee. The ladies had done so much for the Battalion, had shown them so much kind consideration, that the officers and men were quite at their wits end in devising something in recognition. It was first thought that a *soiree dansante* would be a pleasant thing but that idea was abandoned in favor of a promenade concert because of the limited room on the Lee. The tickets were distributed at the prominent city clubs and hotels and among representative business men. They were used simply as a means of controlling in a measure the attendance and were entirely complimentary.

The ticket read like this:

RECEPTION AND PROMENADE CONCERT
TENDERED THE
LADIES OF NEW ORLEANS,
BY THE
Officers and Members of the Seventy-first New York Infantry,
ON BOARD STEAMER ROBERT E. LEE,
Thursday Evening, March 3d,
From 2 until 4 o'clock.
ADMIT GENTLEMAN AND LADIES.

The Concert was a success in every way. The band took a position in the centre of the saloon and chairs were placed as close together as possible from one end of the boat to the other. The attendance was simply enormous and included the elite of those gathered to witness the Carnival festivities as well as residents of the Crescent City. There were scores of men and women present whose names were familiar at every Southern fire-side—distinguished in politics, literature, arts, professions and in society. It was a grand compliment to the Northern regiment—an unprecedented compliment to any organization and appreciated as such. After the concert the ladies took considerable pleasure in examining the quarters of the men. Each overcoat and knapsack was in place and the cabins in perfect order. When the Governors of Louisana and Kentucky and prominent Southern generals—and there were not a few of them—arrived, the guard was turned out and all military honors paid. General Beauregard of course was a marked figure and when he entered the saloon and was ushered to the upper end, where Colonel Vose received the prominent guests, there was a perfect storm of applause. The men cheered and the ladies clapped their hands and waved their dainty handkerchiefs. Beauregard smiled and bowed again and again in response. Some one said something about Bull Run and an old veteran of the Seventy-first jumped to his feet and shouted across the room to the General:

"I was there in sixty-one General."

Beauregard smiled again and held out his hand, which the "vet" enthusiastically clasped. Some of the men induced the General to sit down at a table and write his name on cards and he worked patiently for half an hour. By that time everybody wanted one and he promised to send a number of autographs to New York later, which promise he faithfully kept.

This affair and the serenade to the ladies at the St. Charles Hotel were very great social successes and redounded to both the credit of the regiment and the band. The latter did particularly well at the serenade. The front of the honse was brilliantly illuminated and the balconies thronged with ladies and gentlemen. The evening air was so balmy that no one thought of wraps.

The doors and windows were all open and one passed freely in and out. It was like an August night at home.

"All is gentle; naught
Stirs rudely; but, congenial with the night,
Whatever walks is gliding like a spirit."

This perfect weather came straight from Araby the Blest and did not vary during the Battalion's stay. No travellers were ever more fortunate in the matter of weather or in any other way for the matter of that. The evenings were so delightful that they were often spent sitting in some private garden, bareheaded and in the lightest possible clothing, the aroma of the cigars mingling with the perfumes of the flowers and shrubs, or, on the deck of the Robert E. Lee, watching the puffing monsters splashing their stern wheels in the silvery moon-tinted waters of the river. When the men were wandering about the city very many of them were seized upon by kind hearted citizens, made the heroes of home circles and sent back to quarters loaded with favors of all kinds. Many a quiet, unpretentious citizen opened his heart and house in honor of the blue uniform.

"Therein, he them full fair did entertain,
Not with such forged shows as fitter been
For courting fools, that courtesies would fain
But with entire affection and appearance plain."

CHAPTER XII.

A TRIUMPHANT RETURN.

"Farewell! a word that must be and hath been—
A sound which makes us linger;——yet——farewell."

"'Tis sweet to know there is an eye will mark
Our coming, and look brighter when we come."

Byron.

ON Friday morning early, the resounding rat tat of the drums aroused the dreaming soldier, and with first consciousness came the thought that in an hour or so the merry City was to be left behind—perhaps for ever. It was not a pleasant thought in some respects for many had

learned to like the ways of the *dolce far niente* life they
had been leading, and again, it was a pleasant thought,
for were they not returning home to the frost and the
snow, the crowded streets and the busy marts of the metropolis? To the loved ones they had almost forgotten amid
the smiles and favors of the fair ones of the South ? Many
a heart beat anxiously as the moment of departure came
and regretted that more letters had not been written and
sent North. Epistolary efforts had been few and feeble ;
every one was "so busy you know" and they would be
"so soon back." Telegrams like this took the place of
letters :

New Orleans, February 27th, 1881.

Mrs. John Smith,
    New York City.
        Read the newspapers. Too busy to write. Charming
weather here. JOHN SMITH.
    10 Paid.

They were not all answered like this however :

New York City, February 28.

Mr. John Smith,
    Seventy-first Infantry,
        New Orleans.
        Thanks, will do as you suggest. Weather here very
cold but city very gay indeed. Charming socials nightly. Telegraph
sure when coming home or might be out. Too busy to write. Au
Revoir. MRS. JOHN SMITH.
    33 Collect.

When the Battalion marched out of the boat and away
towards the cars, it was with a joyousness tempered with
a certain sadness at leaving so pleasant quarters. The

officers of the Lee dipped the flags and jingled the great bell on the upper deck, while the whistles of the tugs and steamers in the vicinity set up a roar that drowned out everything except the echoes sent back by the great cotton warehouses flanking the Levee. Early as it was, the streets through which the Battalion marched, were not deserted. The rattle of the drums and the bursts of melody from the band foretold their coming and the men were greeted on every corner by citizens, who, in rising at such an hour to honor their parting guests, paid them more than an empty compliment. From many a laticed casement fair rounded arms waved salutes and from many a door step come a hearty wish of *bon voyage!* The Washington Artillery were drawn up about the depot, and their pieces were bright and shining under the morning sun. Adieus were said, hands clasped for the twentieth time, and the train moved slowly off, the cannons booming a last farewell!

The route was a familiar one, and the party spent the first hour or so in settling themselves comfortably, rather than looking at the panorama of the Mississippi that unfolded itself as they passed northward. Hammond, the scene of the first reception was soon reached, and the familiar faces about the station welcomed as old friends. The men left the train and thoroughly enjoyed the half hour spent in the pretty little hamlet of which they had such pleasant memories. The darkies, as usual, flocked about the cars and asked many questions. One little fellow sided up to Dr. Bryant and said:

" Golly, how many is dey ob you'ns ? "

"Quite a good many, don't you think so ? " responded the Doctor with a smile.

"Dey muss miss you up Norf mighty. Reckon dey muss miss you suah ! "

Some poor fellow who wanted to go North, had found an overcoat and cap in New Orleans where they had been left by some careless member of the detachment. After the special train had left, he put on the coat and hat and went to Mr. Coleman the General Passenger Agent of the Jackson route, to whom he said he was a member of the regiment and wanted to be sent on by the regular passenger train which followed the Special about an hour. A despatch was sent to those on the Special train inform- ing them that one of the party had been left behind. An immediate and very thorough counting of noses, showed that the man was an imposter, and word to that effect was sent to New Orleans by telegraph. It is hardly necessary to say that he did not come North on the passenger train.

The train rumbled on through Louisiana, Tennessee, Mississippi and Kentucky and flowers and smiles awaited it at every station. Invitations came by telegraph from all sides. Grenada wanted the party to dine, but, unfor- tunately the invitation was not received until after the Battalion had reached New York, unintentionally delayed by some gentlemen in New Orleans. Everywhere along the route, congratulations were showered on the party. At dusk, the budding foliage of the South was fast fading away, and it was growing colder hour by hour. In the morning the men awoke, to find ice and snow in Illinois.

> "Now no plumed throng
> Charms the wood with song ;
> Ice bound trees are glittering,
> Merry snow birds twittering
> Fondly strive to cheer
> Scenes so cold and drear."

The men were fortified for the night by a good supper at Vincennes, Indiana, given by Mr. C. S. Cone, Jr., representing the Ohio and Mississippi railroad. They were very tired when night came, and slept well, for

> "Weariness
> Can snore upon the flint, when restive sloth
> Finds the down pillow hard."

Cincinnati was reached about midnight. Everything was quiet and cars were changed in the same depot. The men were soon asleep again and the train rattled on to Grafton, West Virginia, where a warm breakfast waited. Then the party prepared to view the Alleghanies over which they had had so terrible a ride on the memorable "first night out." The scenery was superb as vista after vista unfolded itself to the delighted travellers. They reached the foot—

> "Of the crown'd Alleghany, when he wrapped
> His purple mantle gloriously around
> And took the homage of the princely hills.
> And then in glorious pomp, the sun retired
> Behind that solemn shadow. And his train
> Of crimson and of azure and of gold
> Went floating up the zenith, tint on tint,
> And ray on ray, 'till all the concave caught
> His parting benediction."

On the summit the Cleveland Greys returning from the inauguration of the President to whom they had acted as a body guard, were met and the two organizations saluted each other and exchanged news. It was Sunday, and the Chaplain determined that the fact should not be forgotten. So it was decided that at Cumberland, Maryland, where the Battalion was to be dined by the Baltimore and Ohio Railroad, a service should be held. The dinner at Cumberland was considered one of the pleasantest features of the return. The large hotel there has a very spacious dining room and magnificent piazzas extending the full length of the house. The men were marched into the dining room and seated at tables that seemed particularly inviting after the long ride. Meanwhile the piazzas were thronged with ladies and gentlemen and from the moment of arrival the crowd increased steadily. The dinner was a good one and presided over by Messrs. Lord and Superintendent Spencer of the Railroad Company, who made complimentary speeches and drank in flowing bumpers the health of the Battalion. Immediately after dinner, service was announced, and as many of the Cumberlanders wanted to participate, it was decided that the dining room was probably the best place in which to hold it. So the doors were opened and the people came in and mingled with the boys in blue. It was a curious scene. The chaplain stood at one end of the room. Behind him were a few officers, in front of him the band acting as choir, behind the band was the con-

gregation proper, while all about were the tables covered
with dishes and the remains of the dinner. The "choir"
played the music of the Sweet Bye and Bye and the vast
audience sang the words. Then, Dr. Martin read the 136th
Psalm and prayed for the welfare of the detachment, giving thanks for the past, and trusting in the "Giver of all
good" for the future. In his sermon the Chaplain took
for his text: "Add to your faith virtue, and to virtue knowledge, and to knowledge temperance, and to temperance
godliness, and to godliness brotherly kindness, and to
brotherly kindness charity." Dr. Martin probably never
had so curious an audience, but he grasped the situation
thoroughly and made a success of what with many men,
would have been a failure. It was no slight task to interest such an audience and keep them interested, but the
Chaplain did it.

> " No notes were there :
> No, not a scrap.   All was intuitive
> Pouring like water from a flashing fountain
> With current unexhausted."

He emphasized each of the words of the text as a con-
stituent element of true manhood. The sermon was exceedingly practical, and continuous applications were
made to the circumstances in which the command found
itself. Faith he defined as the power to apprehend the
unseen. Virtue meant manliness, and the importance of
this element was dwelt on especially in the military connection. Knowledge in a republican country was the
keystone of the arch. The old theory was that the peo-

ple were born saddled and bridled, to be ridden by rulers booted and spurred to ride. Our theory is government of, from and by the people. When Russia educates she does it from benevolence; we educate from necessity. Intelligence is the only possible basis of republicanism. No man wants to hold his property at the will of a mob like that of Athens, or his life on the verdict of a Neapolitan jury. Temperance was defined as meaning self-control. If this quality was wholly wanting man would be as much worse than the tiger as his capacity for mischief was greater—a human infernal machine. Godliness meant reverence. If there was a God, a creator of nature and man, then it must be seemly to stand toward Him in a reverential attitude. Brotherly kindness was referred to as having been exemplified in the behavior of the men toward each other during the trip and by the hearty reception accorded them *en route* and in the South. The last quality spoken of as essential to a noble character was charity or love. This was explained as meaning the fulfilling of all the relationships of life in a spirit of good will toward men.

When he finished speaking that grand old tune "America" was played and the chorus rang out from a thousand throats.

When the tired soldiers opened their eyes the next day the waters of the Hudson were rustling at their feet, and the spires and towers of the metropolis were beconing a welcome through the mists of the morning. Once across

the river, the scenes recalled war times when the regiments were temporarily returning from the front. The
down town streets were literally packed with people, and
the Battalion was forced to take the sidewalk as far as
Broadway. The march to the armory was a march of
triumph. Smiles and cheers awaited the men on every
corner. Flags were flying from houses and windows.
The great heart of the metropolis beat in unison with the
cadenced step of the returning invaders, for " Peace hath
her victories, no less renowned than war."

THE END.

APPENDIX.

A.

OFFICIAL RECOGNITION.

In order to reach New Orleans from New York by land, it was necessary to pass through a number of states. Following are the replies sent in response to the official request for permission to pass and repass with arms :

STATE OF NEW JERSEY,
OFFICE OF ADJUTANT GENERAL,
TRENTON, February 1st, 1881.

GEN'L FREDERICK TOWNSEND,
    Adjutant General of New York,
        Albany, N. Y.

General:
    I am directed by his Excellency, Governor George C. Ludlow, to inform you that permission is granted a detachment of the Seventy-First Regiment, National Guard of New York, to pass through the State of New Jersey, armed and equipped, en-route to and return from New Orleans, La. between the 21st of February, and 6th of March, 1881.

Respectfully,
[Signed]   WILLIAM S. STRYKER,
Adjutant General of New Jersey.

COMMONWEALTH OF PENNSYLVANIA,
ADJUTANT GENERAL'S OFFICE,
HARRISBURG, February 1st, 1881.

MAJOR GEN'L FREDERICK TOWNSEND,
   Adjutant General of New York,
      Albany, N. Y.

General:

    Permission is hereby granted a detachment of the Seventy-First Regiment, National Guard, State of New York, to enter and pass through the State of Pennsylvania, armed and equipped, when en-route to New Orleans, La., between February 21st and March 6th, 1881.

        By Command of HENRY M. HOYT,
          Governor and Commander-in-Chief.
          [Signed]   JAMES W. LATTA,
                    Adjutant General.

STATE OF MARYLAND,
ADJUTANT GENERAL'S OFFICE,
ANNAPOLIS, February 1st, 1881.

Special Orders }
  No. 6.   }

    Permission is hereby granted to the Seventy-First Regiment, National Guard, State of New York, to pass through Maryland, armed and equipped, between February 21st and March 6th, 1881.

        By order of the
          Governor and Commander-in-Chief,
          [Signed]   J. WESLEY WATKINS,
                    Adjutant General.

STATE OF DELAWARE,
OFFICE OF ADJUTANT GENERAL
WILMINGTON, DEL., February 1st, 1881.

MAJOR GEN'L F. TOWNSEND,
   Adjutant General of New York,

Sir:

    Yours of 29th ult. duly received, and your request "that permission be granted a detachment of the Seventy-First Regiment, National Guard of the State of New York, to pass through the State of Delaware armed and equipped, en-route to and returning from New Orleans, La., between the 21st of February and the 6th of March, is hereby granted.

        Very respectfully yours,
          [Signed]   J. PARKE POSTLES,
                    Adjutant General of Delaware.

STATE OF WEST VIRGINIA,
OFFICE OF ADJUTANT GENERAL,
WHEELING, February 3d, 1881.

ADJUTANT GENERAL OF NEW YORK,
Albany, N. Y.

General:

In reply to yours of the 29th, asking permission for a detachment of the Seventy-First Regiment, National Guard of your State to pass through the State of West Virginia, I have to say that the same is granted.

Very respectfully,
Your Obedient Servant,
[Signed]   E. L. WOOD,
Adjutant General.

GENERAL HEADQUARTERS, STATE OF OHIO,
Adjutant General's Office,
Columbus, January 31st, 1881.

Special Orders,)
No. 7.   )

Permission is hereby granted the Seventy-First Regiment, National Guard, State of New York, to pass through the State of Ohio, armed and equipped, en-route to and returning from New Orleans, La., between the 21st day of February and the 6th day of March, A. D., 1881.

By order of the Governor.
[Signed]   W. H. GIBSON,
Adjutant General.

OFFICE OF ADJUTANT GENERAL,
State of Tennessee,
Nashville, February 1st, 1881.

TO THE ADJUTANT GENERAL,
State of New York,
Albany, N. Y.

Sir:

By virtue of the authority vested in me as Adjutant General of the State of Tennessee, permission as per your request of the 27th ult., is hereby granted to a detachment of the Seventy-First Regiment, National Guard of the State of New York, to pass and repass, peaceably, through this State, armed and equipped as a military body.

Very respectfully,
Your ob'd't servant,
[Signed]   ERNEST HAWKINS,
Adjutant General of Tennessee.

STATE OF MISSISSIPPI,
Executive Department,
Jackson, February 3d. 1881.

MAJOR GEN'L. FRED'K TOWNSEND,
Adjutant Gen'l New York.
Albany, N. Y.

General:

I have the honor to acknowledge receipt of your communication of the 29th inst., in which you ask permission for a detachment of Seventy-first Regiment, National Guard of New York, to pass through the State of Mississippi, as an armed body, en-route to New Orleans, La., between 21st February and 6th March, 1881, returning again to New York, and to say in reply, and with the sanction of His Excellency, the Governor, that the permission you ask is hereby accorded.

Very respectfully,
[Signed]   A. M. NELSON,
Brig. Gen'l and Adjt. Gen'l Mississippi.

STATE OF KENTUCKY,
Office of Adjutant General,

Special Orders, }   Frankfort, January 31st, 1881.
No. 6.   }

I   At the request of the Adjutant General of the State of New York, permission is granted the Seventy-first Regiment, National Guard, State of New York, or any company or detachment thereof, to enter and pass through the State of Kentucky, armed and equipped, as a military body, en-route to New Orleans, La., and return during February and March proxims. All good citizens of this commonwealth are enjoined to treat them with marked courtesy during such transit.

By command of LUKE P. BLACKBURN, Governor.
[Signed]   J. P. NUCKALS,
Adjutant General.

STATE OF LOUISIANA,
Adjutant General's Office.
New Orleans, February 3d, 1881.

MAJOR GEN'L F. TOWNSEND,
Adjutant General,
Albany, State of New York.

[Extract.]

General:

The permission asked in your communication of 29th inst. is granted as requested, to the Detachment of Seventy-first Regiment Infantry * * of your State Militia, to cross and recross the State of Louisiana, armed and equipped as military bodies.

By order of Commander-in-Chief,
Gov. G. T. BEAUREGARD,
Adjutant General.
[Signed]   A. W. TONTANT BEAUREGARD,
In charge.

APPENDIX B.

.

THE Battalion was the recipient of invitations of all kinds, from the moment of departure until the return. Many of these were sent by telegraph and mail, and all of them were appreciated as the generous offerings of kindly regard. The following are only a few, arranged without regard to date:

HEADQUARTERS FIRST DIVISION
LOUISIANA STATE NATIONAL GUARD,
New Orleans, 22d January, 1881.

COL. RICHARD VOSE,

Commanding Seventy-first Regiment, New York State National Guard, New York City.

Colonel:

I am directed by Major Gen'l W. J. Behan, commanding this Division, in behalf of the officers and men of his command, to extend to your Regiment an invitation to visit our city and participate in the celebration of the approaching Twenty-second of February and Mardi Gras.

General Behan desires to assure you that not only his command, but the citizens generally of New Orleans, will have sincere pleasure in welcoming you and in striving to render pleasant to you a visit which he feels will be national, and its significance as demonstrating that the day of sectionalism in our country is past, and that the extreme South can hospitably and cordially entertain the soldiers of the Empire State and the great metropolis.

I have the honor to be, Colonel.

Very respectfully your obedient servant,

G. A. WILLIAMS,

Col. A. A. G.

DEPARTMENT OF FINANCE,
CITY HALL.

New Orleans, March 2d, 1881.

COL. RICHARD VOSE,

Commanding Seventy-first Regiment,

Now visiting New Orleans.

Colonel:

On behalf of the Committee of the City Government to afford our visiting Military guests and their accompanying friends, an opportunity to visit the "Jetties," I beg leave to herewith send you and your command, as souvenirs, invitations, &c., to said excursion.

We much regretted your gallant command were not with us on the occasion.

Should any of your Regiment, officers or men—or friends—be omitted among the invitations, please notify me and I will at once send invitations, &c.

Respectfully,

THEO. SHUTE,

Secretary of Committee and Colonel L. S. N. G.

OFFICE OF NEW ORLEANS CITY R. R. CO.,

124 CANAL STREET,

New Orleans, March 2d, 1881.

COL. RICHARD VOSE,

Col. Commanding Seventy-first.

Dear Sir:

We hereby tender yourself and command a Special Train for a complimentary trip to and from West End, at any hour, on any day you may be pleased to designate. Sincerely hoping you will accept this invitation, as we desire to render your stay in our Crescent city as pleasant as possible, we have the honor to be,

Very respectfully yours,

FRED. WINTZ, *President,*

C. R. EVANS, *Superintendent.*

HEADQUARTERS COMPANY "A," CONTINENTAL GUARDS,
ODD FELLOW'S HALL,

New Orleans, February 27th, 1881.

To the Officers and Members of }
Seventy-first Regiment, N. Y. S. N. G. }

Gentlemen:

You are most cordially invited to visit our Armory
during your stay in the city.

Will be most pleased to meet you at any time.

Respectfully yours,

WM. PIERCE,

Captain.

ROOMS OF THE PHUNNY PHORTY PHELLOWS,

New Orleans, February 28th, 1881.

To the Officers and Members of }
Seventy-First Regiment, N. Y. S. N. G. }

Gentlemen:

At a meeting of the Association P. 40 P., you were
elected honorary members of that Association, to be known as Mikados
of Gotham. It was the intention of the Association, to make a formal
presentation, but lack of time rendered it impossible.

The uniforms of your Company will afford access to the Ball.

Hoping you will grace the ball with your presence, I remain,

Yours, &c.,

KICKAPOO,

K. of R.

Grenada, Miss., February 28th, 1881.

Capt. Com'd'g Detachment Seventy-first Reg't,

N. Y. National Guards,

New Orleans.

Dear Sir:

Our prominent citizens are desirous that your Com-
mand stop at our town, on your return, two or three hours, if you can
make your arrangements conveniently to do so, and partake of a dinner
we purpose preparing for the occasion.

I am deputed to extend the invitation to you and trust you can accept. We will give you a real Southern welcome.

Please wire your reply and oblige,

Yours truly, &c.,

E. J. LOWENSTEIN.

THE JEFFERSONVILLE DEPOT OF THE QUARTERMASTER'S DEPARTMENT.

Jeffersonville, Ind., February 25th, 1881.

COLONEL RICHARD VOSE,
Seventy-first Regiment, N. Y. N. G.

Colonel:

I have the honor to extend to you and your Command an invitation to visit the Jeffersonville Depot of the Quartermaster's Department of the United States Army.

If, upon your return from New Orleans, you can make it convenient to accept this invitation, your train can be placed upon a side track at this depot.

A cordial welcome will be extended to you and I am convinced that you will be gratified with a visit to this immense Government establishment.

With sentiments of the higest regard,

I am, Colonel, very respectfully.

Your obedient servant,

JAMES A. EKIN,
Deputy Quartermaster General, U. S. Army,
in charge of Depot.

HEADQUARTERS FIFTH REGIMENT INFANTRY,
N. G., S. N. Y.,
No. 8 BEACH STREET,

New York, February 24th, 1881.

COLONEL RICHARD VOSE,
Commanding Detachment Seventy-first Infantry,
New Orleans, La.

Colonel:

I have the honor herewith to tender you an escort to the Detachment of your Command, now on a visit to New Orleans, upon their return home.

If accepted, will you kindly communicate with me the day and hour you expect to arrive in New York City, in time for me to issue the necessary orders.

I have the honor to be, Colonel,

Very respectfully, your obedient servant,

CHARLES S. SPENCER,
Colonel Commanding Fifth Regiment.

[Telegram.]

New York, March 2d, 1881.

C. P. CRAIG,
St. Charles Hotel:

Mr. Garrett and myself extend our hearty congratulations to the officers of the Seventy-first Regiment upon the most gratifying reception they have met with and extend to them an invitation to accept of our hospitality at the Queen City Hotel, Cumberland. Every effort will be made to make their return trip over our line both agreeable and pleasant.

C. K. LORD.

APPENDIX C.

THE TIME TABLE.

THE Battalion left New York at 11 A. M. on Thursday, February 24th and arrived at New Orleans on Sunday Morning, February 27th. The time schedule was as follows :

Leave New York,	Thursday,	February 24th,		11 00 a. m.
Arrive Philadelphia,	"	"	"	2 00 p. m.
" Baltimore,	"	"	"	4 30 "
" Relay,	"	"	"	5 25 "
" Washington,	"	"	"	6 10 "
" Cumberland,	"	"	"	10 50 "
" Grafton,	Friday	February 25th,		3 45 a. m.
" Parkersburg,	"	"	"	7 00 "
" Chillicothe	"	"	"	9 30 "
" Cincinnati,	"	"	"	1 00 p. m.
Leave Cincinnati	"	"	"	5 00 "
Arrive Odin,	Saturday,	February 26th,		2 00 a. m.
" Cairo,	"	"	"	6 15 "
" Milan,	"	"	"	1 30 p. m.
" Jackson, Tenn.	"	"	"	2 30 "
" Grand Junction,	"	"	"	4 30 "
" Holly Springs,	Saturday,	February 25th,		5 40 "
" Water Valley	"	"	"	7 45 "
" Grenada	"	"	"	9 25 "
" Canton,	Sunday,	February 27th,		1 05 a. m.
" Jackson, Miss.	"	"	"	2 05 "
" McComb City,	"	"	"	5 40 "
" Hammond,	"	"	"	8 00 "
" New Orleans,	"	"	"	10 45 "

OFFICERS OF NEW ORLEANS BATTALION.

RICHARD VOSE, Colonel.   EDWIN A. McALPIN, Major.
JOSEPH D. BRYANT, M. D., Major and Surgeon.
CARLOS MARTYN, D. D., Captain and Chaplain.
F. H. JORDAN, 1st Lieutenant and Acting Adjutant.
ORRIN C. HOFFMAN,
Captain, Inspector of Rifle Practice and Acting Quartermaster.
JACOB HESS,
1st Lieutenant and Commissary of Subsistence.

First Company.
A. W. BELKNAP, Captain Commanding,
GEORGE W. MILLS, Lieutenant,
F. J. McDONALD, First Sergeant.

Second Company.
S. G. BLAKELEY, Captain Commanding,
T. P. PARKS,* Lieutenant,
M. B. ENGLE, First Sergeant,

Third Company,
JOHN F. COWAN, Captain Commanding.
FRANK T. L. GENET, Lieutenant,
G. B. HEBARD, First Sergeant.

Fourth Company.
J. A. TAYLOR, Captain Commanding,
GEORGE G. MILNE, Lieutenant,
WILLIAM HAMILTON, First Sergeant.

Sergeant Major, FREDERICK KOHNEN; Quartermaster's Sergeants, GEORGE VANNESS and DUNCAN B. HARRISON; Commissary Sergeants, JOHN HAGADORN, FRED. MAY and JAMES KENNEDY; Ordnance Sergeant, GEORGE REINHARDT; Hospital Steward, JULIUS IMGARD; Colonel's Orderly, EDMUND ALBERT; Drum Major, NAT. T. JENKS; Band Master, MORRIS J. JOYCE. Sergeant Standard Bearers, J. B. SCOTT and MILTON VOSBURGH; Right General Guide, E. B. ST. JOHN HENRIQUES; Left General Guide, FREDERICK MAY.

THE KING'S BANNER.

The Banner truly deserves minute description when one takes notice of the great amount of time and labor expended upon it.

It is forty-three (43) inches wide and thirty-three (33) inches deep. The front of it is made of three different colors. The upper right hand corner being of heavy green satin, and the lower left hand corner of royal purple Satin de Leon. Running diagonally across is a stripe of cloth of gold, 13½ inches wide, which is very beautifully embroidered. In the direct centre of the band is a crown composed of gold embroided cardinal, gold velvet and jewels. Exactly in the top centre of the crown is a small cross, with a large diamond in the middle. The cross rests upon a gold ball, from under which come five (5) bands of gold embroidery which are fastened on to the head band by five (5) large rubies. Between each of the bands are three (3) pearls, set upon cardinal velvet to form a triangle. The head band of the crown is of gold embroidery, having in the centre

*Deceased.

a large garnet cut in diamond shape and surrounded by four (4) small rubies. On either side of the centre is a diamond presumably about the size of a pigeon's egg. And again upon the left and right of each diamond is an emerald, corresponding in size and shape with the centre garnet and also surrounded by four (4) rubies. The crown is lined with blue velvet. It is from the top of the cross to the crown edge of the head band 7½ inches and is at the widest part 8¾ inches. The cross is surrounded by a wreath of laurals, myrtle and acorns, interspersed here and there with berries made of small rubies. The sprays are confined together with a silver ribbon, (embroidered) the ends each having two (2) emeralds set in, and the centre knots have a large ruby. The embroidery is very handsome.

The reverse side of the banner is of blue silk in the centre of which is a handsomely painted copy of the regimental badge, which is a gold belt and buckle, upon which in letters of black is the Seventy-first's motto, "PRO ARIS ET PRO FOCIS." The other space in the middle of the belt is a monogram of 71 and A. G. (American Guard), and an extra addition of *Rex* 1881 is directly under the monogram. The edge of the entire banner is finished with a heavy gold bullion fringe 2½ inches deep and headed with gold lace an inch deep. The banner is hung by gold loops upon a gold cross bar forty-five (45) inches long, each end of which has upon it a gold filagree crown, the band of which has in it four (4) medium sized diamonds between each of which is a large stone, each different. One (1) ruby, (1) saphire, (1) emerald and (1) amethyst. There are four (4) ivy leaves standing erect from these bands and in the centre of each is an odd stone corresponding with those in the band. Between each ivy leaf is a large pearl. The crowns are 12½ inches broad and 3¼ inches high.

The standard upon which the bar hangs is surmounted by a very large silver ball upon which is perched a spread eagle. Upon this eagle's head rests a very diminutive crown. Around the centre of the silver ball is a gold filagree band, from the top of which rise four other filagree pieces which meet under the eagle's feet. In the band running around the ball are set eight (8) large stones, alternating rubies and diamonds and in the four (4) other gold pieces are in each a large emerald. Directly below the ball and upon the standard is a heavy bow formed of the three (3) colors of the front of the banner. It is made of heavy gros grain ribbon and is fastened with a large gold star. Underneath this again is secured a heavy gold cord which is draped to the crowns of the cross-bar and from that depend almost to the ground. The ends of this cord are finished with gold bullion balls and tassels.

The stones or jewels in the banner are very numerous, there being:

15 Diamonds,
39 Rubies,
14 Emeralds,
4 Garnets,
4 Amythists,
4 Sapphires,
21 Pearls,
Making in all, 111 stones.

The standard upon which the banner is hung is 9 feet 3 inches high, from the crown on the eagle-head to the ground.

APPENDIX D.

ODDS AND ENDS.

It would be impossible to print the thousand and one notices of the Battalion's trip or the peculiar communications received by the officers on all conceivable subjects. The limited collection of odds and ends subjoined will no doubt prove interesting.

A RELIC OF THE WAR.

On card bearing clasped hands at the top are two buttons. One is the Louisiana State button with the Pelican in relief. The other is a New York State button dimmed and moulded by time. On the card is inscribed:

COLONEL RICHARD VOSE,

Please accept these buttons as a souvenir of your welcome visit—one is from my Confederate uniform, the other was taken from that of a New York soldier in Virginia. They are now the symbol of the mutual love of fair Louisiana and generous New York.

"Once foes in war, now in peace true friends again."

Fraternally yours,

CHARLES E. CAYLAT,

Veteran Washington Artillery.

Mr. Caylat also sends a number of verses entitled "The Lone Star Flag," and dedicated to "General J. Bankhead Magruder; C. S. A," to be sung to the air of the "Bonnie Blue Flag." At the top of the sheet on which they are printed is the red white and red flag crossed with one of blue bearing the "lone star." The verses were printed in New Orleans January, 1863, but bear the imprint of Richmond, Virginia, in order that Mr. Caylat the author, might "avert" himself "from the tender mercies of Ben Butler." It is the last copy of the edition. The verses are firey enough if not of the highest poetical order. The first runs like this:

"Mount, mount and speed away to Louisiana's prairies wide,
Th' avenging sword is our sceptre, the fleet steed our pride;
Raise up! 'our lone star flag,' let its single star gleam out,
Mount! mount! and speed away, put the Yan-kees to rout."

KINDLY WARNING.

The following despatch received en route was no doubt kindly meant but as the route advised had already been determined on it was of little value:

[Telegram.]
Dated, Evergreen, Ala., Feb. 20, 1881.
Received at 666 Sixth Avenue, Feb. 21.

To COL. VOSE,
Seventy-first Regiment, N. Y.

After reaching Louisville take the Detachment via. Milan to New Orleans. Don't go via. Montgomery and Mobile, road in bad condition.

20 paid ½ rate.   ALEX.

GENERAL BEAUREGARD'S SIGNATURE.
New Orleans, March 5, 1881.

MY DEAR COLONEL,

By to-day's mail I send for some of your officers and men the autographs which they did me the honor of asking while I was on board of the R. E. Lee on the 3d inst. Will you please do me the favor of distributing them.

I trust that you all had a safe and pleasant journey back to New York.

I am, with respect,
Yours very truly,
G. T. BEAUREGARD.

COL. R. VOSE.

A POETIC VETERAN.

A veteran of the Seventy-first in Washington when the Battalion passed through became so enthused that he broke out into rhyme and sent the following to New Orleans on two postal-cards:

(1)   Washington, D. C., Feb. 25, 1881.
1861-81.

I would not if I could forget
That twenty years ago,
On old Virginia's soil I met
And fought a gallant foe.

Who wore the gray and who the blue,
I care not now to say,
For both to cause and flag were true
On that eventful day.

(2)   Our valiant dead sleep where they fell,
Accursed be they, who
Disturb a soldier's grave to tell
If he wore gray or blue.

Now, brothers gray, give me your hand
And swear that ever we
In peace or war together stand,
Union and Liberty!

R. H. CHITTENDEN,
Private, Co. A., N. Y. 71st.

A CONTRAST.

(From Philadelphia Record.)

As your correspondent watched "the boys" march down Broadway yesterday, a whole battalion of the brave dead and of grizzled veterans seemed to accompany them. It will be remembered that the three months' term of the Seventy-first had expired before the first battle of Bull Run, yet they stayed and volunteered for the fight. At 4 o'clock on the morning of July 21, your correspondent sat on horseback on Centreville Heights, this side of Bull Run, waiting for Hunter's Division to pass through and go to the right, when I heard my name called out by one and another, and I turned and found myself surrounded by Seventy-first boys who had halted for a moment. The youths who carried muskets in the command were nearly all of gentle birth and accustomed to luxurious living at home, but they were in rough dress and embrowned with the sun, and seemed full of life and animation. They went into battle as into a holiday, and had no doubt that they would return to New York in triumph by way of Richmond.

A few hours later, as I stood on a caisson of Ayres' Battery, near Bull Run Bridge, at the centre of the line, I saw the Seventy-first emerge from the woods at Sudley Church on the extreme right, in company with the First and Second Rhode Island regiments. They formed a line of battle in an open field, and the New York boys did it as handsomely as they had ever done it on Broadway, and quite as coolly. A few moments and there came a flash, smoke, the report of a volley, then continuous firing, and two horses with empty saddles dashed through the woods close by me, and I could see men carrying off the wounded from the field. I never see the Seventy-first but I think of its record on that day, when so many three months' regiments had gone home; and the battery attached to my own brigade (a New York battery) had left their guns in the morning and marched back to Washington to the music of our guns. Only on such days as yesterday, when old historical associations come up again, does this famous command get something like the attention it deserves. Now, by a singular coincidence, they will be the guests at New Orleans of a committee of eminent citizens headed by General Beauregard, the same soldier who was in command of the Confederate forces at the first Bull Run. He will find that the boys can still stand fire.

"NEW YORK'S FAVORITES."

(New York Mercury Editorial.)

THE CARNIVAL SEASON.—New York ends her carnival season to-morrow night with a grand ball at the Academy of Music, but at New Orleans the festivities will continue until the bells usher in Ash Wednesday. The celebration of Mardi Gras in the latter city distances in splendor and enthusiasm all similar festivities elsewhere, and even the famous carnival at Rome cannot come into comparison. This year the festival will be made even more attractive and brilliant by the presence of the Boston Lancers and our own Seventy-first Regiment. To-day New Orleans welcomes New York's favorite military organization with open arms and will greet them with genuine Southern hospitality. The occasion will not only be one of unalloyed pleasure, but the whole country will be made the happier by its exhibition of fraternal good will. Our city should see to it that the gallant Seventy-first is received on its return with the enthusiastic honors it deserves.

A SOUTHERN WELCOME.

(New Orleans Democrat Editorial.)

The arrival yesterday of the New York Seventy-first Regiment marked another delightful epoch in our season of carnival. The weather was simply perfect, and the spontaneous bursts of applause from the populance that greeted the visiting soldiery from the moment they left the cars until they finally retired from the streets must have told them better than words, however glowing or impassioned, how genuinely glad the people of New Orleans were to have them in their city. It was a pleasant and most inspiring sight to witness the enthusiastic manner in which the Northern soldiers were welcomed on all sides, and our military seemed especially delighted at the opportunity which was presented to testify their appreciation of the honor conferred upon our city by this visit of the soldiers from the Empire State.

Our people are generous, appreciative and demonstrative, and are apt to give quick expressions to their feelings, marked emphasis to their likes and dislikes, and their unrestrained expressions of pleasure and of admiration yesterday must have been gratifying to those whose presence among us on this joyous occasion is the best evidence of their feeling and of their desire to cultivate sentiments of friendship and mutual regard.

We are sure that our people, one and all, will meet them more than half-way, and that they will grasp the hands thus outstretched to them in no uncertain or faltering manner, but with an earnestness and cordiality which will eloquently convey their true sentiments.

OUR BAND CONCERT.

(New Orleans Democrat.)

There were fully 1,000 people at the Washington Artillery arsenal last evening to listen to the music of the band of the Seventy-first New York Regiment. now on a visit to our city. It is so seldom that such a band visits us that our guests' music was certainly delightful, and its ex-

16

ecution accurate and expressive. Our own bands are no mean competitors in instrumentation, but lack, what is so evident in our visiting band, thoroughness of drill and perfection of time.

The concert given last night was a musical treat to those who are connoisseurs in instrumental music, and the effect was peculiarly marked in the cornet pieces. The leader, Mr. M. J. Joyce, shows admirable skill in his control over the band, and his baton is almost as expressive as the instruments under him. The selections were most judiciously made and the enchores were loud and long after each piece. The following was the programme:

Priest's March, "Athalie" (Mendelssohn), overture, "Banditen-streiche" (Suppe); cornet duet, "Leviathan" (Levy), Messrs. Arthur and Fred. W. Bent; sonate adante, "Religieuse" (Volkmar); euphonium solo, "Fantasie" (Kral), Mr. F. Kral; selections, "Ye Olden Times" (Beyer); Xylocalme selections, Mr. Charles Lowe, Jr.; Hallelujah chorus, "Messiah" (Handel); cornet solo, "Young America" (Hartmann), Mr. Fred. W. Bent; romanza, "Palm Branches" (Faure); potpourri, "Pirates of Penzance" (Sullivan); march, "Greeting to Royal Host" (Joyce), dedicated to the members of the "Royal Host."

"WELCOME HOME."
(New York Mercury Editorial.)

WELCOME HOME.—To-morrow the boys of the gallant Seventy-first will come marching home, fresh from the scenes of their patriotic triumphs in the South, and they will receive no doubt a most enthusiastic welcome. Their journey to Louisiana has been one continued ovation, and in the Crescent City they were the receipients of almost regal attention. The regiment that stood up so bravely for the flag that marshaled them to battle, never appeared in a nobler light than on the day last week when they fired a volley over the graves of the confederate dead, in New Orleans' Greenwood Cemetery. It was a touching tribute to foemen worthy of their steel and the highest possible proof of their wish to cement anew the friendly ties that now link the North and South together. One such occasion as this does more to unite all the sections of our common country than all the speeches that could be made on the rostrum. The Seventy-first has made every citizen of New York its debtor.

"WELCOME GUESTS."
(New Orleans Picaune Editorial.)

The expected detachment of the Seventy-First Regiment of New York arrived yesterday to remain until after Mardi Gras. As they marched through some of the principal streets they presented a fine appearance, and were warmly applauded by thousands of people who had gathered to see them. They are most welcome guests, and we have no doubt will be made to feel so notwithstanding the packing together of the immense host of visitors now here: The very jam will force many who were strangers to touch elbows and part friends. Let none lose their good nature because of the jam, let the hive buzz with a cordial welcome, so that all our visitors may return to their homes more than ever heretofore convinced that this, maybe, is a common country after all and that all the people of all the sections, may mingle without animosity and live in the sincere friendship becoming and necessary to every harmonious and really united people.

WHAT CINCINNATI THOUGHT OF THE MARCHING.
(*From Cincinnati Commercial.*)

No time was lost in falling into line in the Plum Street Depot, and as they emerged from it into the open square fronting on the depot, they found the First Regiment, Ohio National Guards, 150 strong, drawn up in single file with presented arms. Either the legs of the visitors were stiffened from long riding, or else the positions were new to many of them, but whatsoever may have been the cause, their distances were badly kept as they marched down the front, nor did matters improve when by companies, they wheeled into Elm street, every platoon doing it with more or less of a curve. The band alone made the turn like the spokes of a wheel. On Elm street the visitors came to a halt and present, while the home regiment, in their clean but time-worn and shabby fatigue uniforms, marched by in perfect alignment, heads up, shoulder to shoulder, with the regularity and precision of veterans. A course was taken east on Fourth street, and then it was that under the inspiriting strains of the magnificent band and the glances of hundreds of Ohio ladies that lined the sidewalks, the Seventy-first improved and was at its best, their attractions being enhanced by the dark blue uniform, with light blue and gold facings, white cross and waist belts, with polished plates, the dark blue being again relieved by white pompons and the red blanket which each man had strapped upon the top of his knapsack. For arms they carried Remington breechloaders, each piece shining like new silver, and the brilliant appearance of the entire command, as it went by way of Fourth and Vine streets to the Esplanade, where their guns were stacked, will long be remembered.

EARLY HISTORY.
(*From Cincinnati Commercial.*)

The Seventy-first was originally organized nearly fifty years ago, but under another name. In 1861 Colonel Abraham Vosburg made of it an exclusively American Guard, and for the first time the New York Seventh had all it could do to retain its laurels, and since that year keeping its position with difficulty. Colonel Vosburg's command went among the earliest to the seat of war and his regiment was the one that stood the brunt of Bull Run and left the field as if on dress parade. They lost heavily. On returning from thirty days' service they furnished to other regiments a larger proportion of officers in proportion to their numerical strength than any other organization in New York. Brave General Winthrop was a graduate of the Seventy-first. The present Colonel, Richard Vose, has held his present position for nine years, and been in active service in the rebellion and at home for twenty-six years. He is an iron disciplinarian, and loves his command as if they were his own children.

THE PROMENADE CONCERT ON BOARD THE R. E. LEE.

(From New Orleans Picayune.)

Yesterday afternoon, from two to half-past four o'clock, a reception was held by the Seventy-first Regiment on board the steamer, R. E. Lee. The splendid cabin was thronged with ladies and gentlemen during the whole of this period, and they were elegantly entertained by the New York boys in blue.

The regimental band under the direction of the youthful, but talented leader, M. J. Joyce, delighted the auditors with a concert. Deserving of special mention, was the Euphonium solo, by F. Kral, and the cornet solos, by Arthur and Fred Bent, particularly the duet from the Donjon scene from Trovatore.

During the afternoon, Gen. G. T. Beauregard paid a visit to the boat and was received with military honors at the landing, and with cheers from the members of the Seventy-first upon his entering the cabin.

The reception was of an informal character and was hearty, not to say enthusiastic.

The Seventy-first leaves this morning for New York. The members have made many friends here, both among the fair sex and the masculine portion of the community, and have much enjoyed their visit to the Crescent City.

A DINNER WE DID'NT GET.

While the train was *en route* to Cincinnati, a card was shown bearing a very elegant *menu* and very elegant printed covers. It was regarded with more or less curiosity and no one pretended to know what it meant. The following extract from the *Cincinnati Commercial* explains the whole matter satisfactorily to all except those who are credited with eating the dinner. The *Commercial* says after quoting the *menu* : "The boys filled their blue uniforms until they threatened to part." Had any such dinners been served that would have been true no doubt, but alas, all that was seen of the repast was the following bill of fare. The *Commercial* says :

"Before reaching Philadelphia, and when the majority of the command were wishing they had brought a snack along, the following *menu* on handsomely tinted folio cards with silhouette embellishments, were handed around."

Oysters on half shell.	[Chablis.]
Potage.	
Green Turtle.	[Amontillado.]
Poisson.	
Savannah Shad.	[Rudelsheimer.]
Entrees	

Ris de Veau Financiere,

Poitrine de Dindonneau.

Farcie a l'impertrat,

[Champagne.]

Froid.

Pate de Strasbourg,

Voliere de Cailles a la Forestierre.
Gibier.

Perdreau Barde,

Coeur de Laitue,

Salade de Celeri,

Entremeuts. [Chambertin]

Petites pois a la Francaise,

Asperges en branches,

Haricots Vert.

[Sautes au Beurre]

Sucres,

Charlotte Russe,

Gelee au Champagne,

Fruits et Dessert.

Fromage, Cafe Cigars.

ACCEPTING THE OLIVE BRANCH.

From the New Orleans Democrat.

The visit of the troops from Boston, and New York city to New Orleans, their participation in our carnival festivities, and the cordial and heartfelt greeting that has been extended to them on the part of our military and people at large is, in our opinion, one of the most auspicious circumstances that has occurred since the standard of the opposing armies were furled in 1865. and the throbbings of the war drums were hushed forever. These gentlemen soldiers who come from the far North, bearing in their hands the olive branch, and in their hearts sentiments of friendship and esteem have, naturally, been received by the citizens of New Orleans with open arms, and it must be a predudiced mind and cold heart indeed that cannot understand the noble spirit that actuates those on both sides who, now that the war is a faded memory, desire to clasp hands like brothers and citizens as they are of a common country, and who, recognizing the manhood and patriotism that inspired the soldiers who wore the blue and the gray, would obliterate all unkind thoughts and embittered memories by mingling with each other on terms of mutual respect and admiration. Our honored guests from the North will be able to return home and say to their people that the soldiers of Louisiana are as true to the Union and as patriotic as those in any part of the entire country; that the wild stories of sectional animosity and social ostracism which they are continually hearing of as existing at the South are the emanations of folly or malice, and that, look as closely as they might, they could discover nothing but sentiments of sincerest friendship, an earnest desire to have Northern and Western men come here and live among our people, and assist them in developing the resources of a soil which is rich beyond the dreams of those who live in less favored portions of the United States. They will, we feel assured, bear testimony that the people of this city and State are not the semi-barbarian and inhuman people they are always described as being by demagogues and paid partisan writers about election times, and that they are as earnestly desirous of peace and good will as those of Massachusetts and New York. We have been led to these remarks by the announcement which is made in another part of the Democrat this morning, that the members of the Seventy-first New York regiment will to-day decorate the Confederate monument in Greenwood cemetery, and pay the ashes of our heroic dead there the honors of war. The war is over, indeed, when representative soldiers of the North can find it in their hearts to treat the graves of their fallen, one time adversaries as they would those of their own lost comrades, and when the soldiers of the Crescent City can stand side by side with the soldiers of Massachusetts on the historic hill where our forefathers met the invading British. We believe that this is the first time since the war that Northern soldiers have visited the South and decorated the graves of the Confederate dead, and we know that the act will be productive of great good—proving to the Southern people that the men of the North are as magnanimous in peace as they found them brave in war. The ceremonies to-day over the confederate monument at Greenwood will doubtless be most interesting and impressive, and should be witnessed by as many of our people as possible. The Seventy-first has won golden opinions from our citizens already, and this graceful act will serve to draw us to them all the more.

OUR DRESS PARADE.
(From a New Orleans Paper.)

Yesterday evening at 5 o'clock, the Seventy-first regiment held dress parade in front of their head-quarters, at the foot of Julia street, opposite the steamer R. E. Lee. The regiment presented a fine, soldierly appearance, in their blue regimentals trimmed with gold and snowy-white pants. The movements of the various companies as they took position in the line showed them to be practiced soldiers, and their formation in double rank gave a solid appearance to the line which is lacking in the single rank formation. Col. Vose is, it seems, very particular about the drill of his regiment, for though (allowances being made for a few slips and some carelessness quite excusable on the day after Mardi Gras) the battalion did well for the first time, he had the ceremony performed several times until perfection was attained by his command. There the admirable discipline of this "corps d'elite" was eminently displayed, and as the companies were dismissed and called back into line, not a murmur was heard, and with steady steps the commands were obeyed. A noticable point in these soldiers is their proudly unconscious bearing in the ranks and their steady look to the front, minding neither right nor left. This shows great discipline and speaks highly in favor of the officers. The line officers deserve special praise for their perfect knowledge of their business and their fine handling of their weapons. The marching in review in double ranks was beautifully done, and some of the wheelings remarkably neat. In fine, the Seventy-first regiment showed last evening, some splendid points, and it was an off-day at best for a serious exhibition of military skill.

The newspapers were very kind to the Battalion, and lavished praise on every thing it did. There was only one instance of severe criticism, and that was in an obscure weekly, and seemed suggestively spiteful, though perhaps it was not entirely undeserved. It was in reference to the dress parade, Wednesday evening, on the Levee. The audience was small, the men tired after the pleasures of Tuesday night and there was, no doubt, a certain looseness in the manuel and marching. No one knew this better than the field and line officers, and in fact the men themselves. Yet, there was no reason for the bitteness of the attack and it seemed as though it was not the outcome of some critical newspaper writer, but rather suggested by petty jealousy on the part of some visitor.

The morning after the Battalion's arrival, the several newspapers published a complete lits of those accompanying it, and recorded the doings of the men daily. Besides this, there was published both in Cincinnati and New Orleans, a number of little squibs that were amusing and interesting. For instance:

"—The New York Times has an able and pleasant representative in the person of Mr. Field L. Hosmer, who is now with the Seventy-first regiment, N. Y. S. N. G., on the steamer R. E. Lee. We hope he will be pleased with the Crescent City.

It is safe to say the hope was realized for Mr. Hosmer *was* pleased.

"—One of the most sympathetic members of the Seventy-first regiment N. Y. S. N. G., is Mr. Norval E. Ford, of the editorial staff of the Baltimore Sun. His paper is highly prized here, and we hope he will be pleased with his trip South.

Mr. Ford had reason to be "sympathetic" because during the war he did gallant service for the " lost cause." He was not a member of the Seventy-first either, but then that did not matter much as he was a welcome guest.

"—Capt. Isaac R. Denman, of Newark, New Jersey, came with the Seventy-first regiment, N. G. S. N. Y., to New Orleans. He is with the regiment on the R. E. Lee."

Captain Denman was a talented representative of the little state that is said to be sinking into the sea and the Battalion was ready at any time to wager a large amount that he could wear more medals and decorations on a given area of cloth than any man south of Mason and Dixon's line.

"—One of the veterans of the Seventy-first New York regiment is Mr. Eugene S. Conklin, of the firm of Mulford Cary & Conklin, No. 34 Spruce street, New York. He resides temporarily on the steamer Robert E. Lee."

That would have cost Mr. Conklin about forty cents a line in New York, but then, after all, what is the use of being a veteran and all that sort of thing if one cannot —— but never mind.

"—Mr. G. H. Fleming, the handsome correspondent of the New York Evening Mail and a member of the Seventy-first regiment, N. Y. S. N. G., is quartered with his regiment on the Robert E. Lee, at the foot of Julia street."

That paragraph made Mr. Fleming's fortune with the ladies, not that they could not see for themselves, of course, but because it was a great thing to have an official backing of that sort.

"—Jacob Hess, Esq., Chairman of the Commissioners of Charities for the City of New York, arrived here yesterday with the Seventy-first, New York, of which regiment he is the Commissary. Mr. Hess was here last Mardi Gras, also, when he made many friends who will be glad to renew their acquaintance with him now."

There is not much to be said about that note. Everybody that meets genial "Jake" once, always wants to meet him again.

"—Somebody sent to General Hickenlooper to request him to make a speech to the visiting regiment at the Gibson House dinner. Great Edison! shouted the Lieutenant Governor, can't a body of men come to this town and get something to eat without being talked to death?"

Govenor Hickenlooper is a wise man in his generation and should be re-elected.

—"That drum major was 'a dandy.' He smiled when the home individuals walked by."

Jenks says that must be a mistake, because he never smiles when on parade.

UNIFORMED VETERANS.

The following gentlemen, members of the Uniformed Veteran Corps, accompanied the Battalion to the South. They attracted much attention and were the recipients of much hospitality.

JOSEPH J. LITTLE,

Enlisted in old 37th, September, 1861. Served until 1869. First Sergeant and mustered out United States service as First Lieutenant.

GEORGE B. RAYNOR.

Enlisted December 12th, 1860. Mustered out, 1869.

EUGENE H. CONKLIN,

Enlisted October 4th, 1861. Mustered out. 1868, as First Sergeant.

CHARLES E. BROWN,

Enlisted October 2d, 1862, Corporal, 1866; Sergeant, 1867; Second Lieutenant, 1869. Mustered out, December 20th, 1873.

APPENDIX E.

RESOLUTIONS.

When the Battalion reached Hammond, Louisiana, a stopping place about fifty miles from New Orleans, it was met by a detachment of the Washington Artillery, and a representation of the Army of the Tennessee. The latter presented the following resolutions elegantly printed on white satin :

HEADQUARTERS ASSOCIATION OF THE ARMY OF⎫
Tennessee, Louisiana Division. ⎬
New Orleans, La., February, 1881. ⎭

With cordial Welcome and Greeting :

Considering the auspicious circumstances under which such a numerous and prominent portion of our military brethren of a Northern State of the Union have favored New Orleans with their presence, and with the view of giving formal expression of our appreciation of the wisdom and patriotism of such fraternization between the citizens of this great republic:

Resolved, That the veterans of the army of Tennessee of the late Confederate States, do extend to you the hand of fellowship. Individually as fellow citizens, and collectively as soldiers, pledged to honor and defend the flag of our country.

Resolved, That this association, entertaining neither bitterness for the past, nor animosity for the future, cherish only recollections of the prowess, devotion and valor of the American soldier wherever exhibited, and hold it in high esteem the glorious record won by your command.

Resolved, That this testimonial is intended that you may bear it with you to your homes as a memento of the high regard and good fellowship in which you are held by the veterans of the Confederacy.

J. A. CHALARON, President.
JOHN AGUSTIN, First Vice-President.
H. N. JENKINS, Second Vice-President.
A. J. LEWIS, Third Vice-President.
JOS. D. TAYLOR, Recording Secretary.
EUGENE MAY, Corresponding Secretary.
ALCIDE BOISBLANC, Financial Secretary.
S. D. STOCKMAN, Treasurer.

HEADQUARTERS BATTALION WASHINGTON ARTILLERY,
New Orleans, March 29th, 1881.

Colonel:

I have the pleasure to advise you, that, by direction of the Battalion Washington Artillery, I shall send to your address by express to-morrow, a copy of the preamble and resolutions unanimously adopted by the Battalion, giving expression of their gratification and satisfaction, resulting from the visit of the representatives of your regiment to this city during the festival season, just passed. The distinct expression of the sentiments of the Battalion, as conveyed in the resolutions, I beg to assure you are sincere as they are pronounced.

I have the honor to be
Most Respectfully,
J. B. WALTON,
Honorary Colonel B. W. A. Chairman.

COL. RICH'D VOSE,
Seventy-first N. Y. S. N. G.
New York, N. Y.

The resolutions referred to in the above letter close as follows :

" We cannot omit to give expression to the admiration of ourselves and our fellow citizens upon the courteous bearing of our honored guests during their short stay with us. They were found as genial and submissive to all demands in peace as they have been found to be valiant, patriotic and devoted in war ; they have endeared themselves now in peace as companions and friends. Their stay with our people has afforded abundant satisfaction, and we have the hope that on their return to their distant homes they will carry with them only pleasant memories. The past is no more ! We invoke for the bright and promising future, peace and kind good will."

APPENDIX F.

THE celebration of " Mardi Gras " was no doubt introduced into New Orleans by Bienville and his followers, at all events the memory of the oldest inhabitant does not extend back to a time when the day was not one of frolic and fun in the Crescent City. It has always been marked by processions of more or less magnitude, and the night by parties and balls and other gay assemblages. The first regularly organized "mystic" society, the now famous "Mystick Krewe of Comus," made their first appearance, Mardi Gras night, February 24th, 1857, illustrating by their gorgeous pageants "Milton's Paradise Lost." It was not until 1872 that His Majesty, the King of the Carnival, the merriest monarch of all the world, assumed sway in New Orleans. About two months before Mardi Gras his first proclamation was issued, and this was followed by numerous orders, which were obeyed with alacrity. The courts were closed, legislature adjourned, the public schools were given a holiday, the Mayor surrendered the city and all public business was suspended in obedience to orders from this august monarch. Strolling bands of maskers had always paraded the streets on Mardi Gras and the first object of His Majesty was to gather these into one grand body and thus make a spectacle worthy of the day. The success of the first year led to greater efforts for the next, and in 1873 the Rex procession was the wonder and admiration of thousands of spectators.

In 1874 His Majesty announced that he would arrive in his chosen Capital on Monday, the day previous to Mardi Gras, and a grand reception worthy of his exalted rank was arranged. Thus, an additional day was added to the season of fun and proved such a thorough success that every year since the King has arrived on Monday, and his reception and escort have become, in pomp and glory, second only to his grand day pageant on the following day Mardi Gras. On that day, in 1874, His Majesty was accompanied by the Shah of Persia and King Boabdill, the last of the Moorish Kings, with magnificent retinues.

The year 1875 is a blank in carnival history, all celebrations having been postponed on account of the lively bubbling of the political cauldron.

In 1876 His Majesty presented his fourth grand day pageant, representing brilliant scenes from Egyptian history, in which Anthony and Cleopatra were shining and leading figures.

In 1877 His Majesty's followers gave their first turn-out on floats in magnificently arranged tableaus, taking for their subject the "history of the military progress of the world."

In 1878 they presented a caricature on Roman and Grecian Mythology, which was a grand success.

In 1879 the subject of the day pageant, in honor of His Majesty, was a comic history of the nations of the world, His Majesty appearing as Richard Coeur de Leon, with a most brilliant suite.

In 1880 His Majesty's procession represented the four elements, earth, air, fire and water, and those who saw it thought it would never be excelled, if ever equalled.

His Majesty proved equal to the popular demands, however, and in 1881, with "Scenes from the Arabian Nights' Tales," quite eclipsed all of his former efforts. Having witnessed this gorgeous moving panorama, it is safe to say that, in extent, in magnificence of costumes and in attention to every detail, the pageant could not have been surpassed in any city of the world, yet we understand that His Majesty's followers are preparing a pageant for 1882 which they are determined shall rank ahead of all former efforts. With them, to resolve is to accomplish, and therefore, a rare treat is in store for those who visit the Crescent City during the Carnival of 1882. His Majesty rules through a regularly organized government, which consists of two houses of parliament, the Royal Host and Carnival Court, and an executive council, the School of Design, composed of members elected by the Royal Host and Carnival Court.

The School of Design, as its name implies, furnishes subjects for the annual pageants, makes all contracts necessary for their organization and annually elects the King, who is taken from one of the two organizations, for extraordinary services rendered to the royal house. The compliment thus conferred is bestowed gratuitously, as a mark of recognition. The School of Design is an incorporated body under the laws of Louisiana.

The Royal Host is composed of the Peers of the Realm Dukes—created by His Majesty—whose titles are conferred as a reward for active and financial services rendered to the royal government. Carnival Court is generally composed of younger men, lawyers, doctors, clerks and students—the embryo "mashers" of the future Crescent City. One can scarcely realize the amount of work devolving upon the chief officials of his Majesty's government, all of which is done "pro bono publico," without money and without price. That enterprising merchant and able financeer Albert Baldwin, Esq., President of the New Orleans National Bank and head of the great hardware firm of A. Baldwin & Co., as the Duke of Massasoit is

President of the Royal Host and presiding officer of the School of Design. James I. Day, Esq., President of the Sun Mutual Insurance Company, of New Orleans, and an old and highly respected resident, as the Duke of Wamphossock is the Custodian of the Royal Purse. The Hon. George H. Braughn, a prominent member of the Louisiana bar and of the legal firm of Braughn, Buck & Dinkelspiel, with great ability and admirable courtesy fills the high and arduous offices Bathurst, Lord High Chamberlain, Earl Marshal of the Empire, and Manager of the School of Design. In the two positions just named he acts as the executive officer of His Majesty, and, as Earl Marshal, he is *ipse facto* the President of Carnival Court. As Manager of the School of Design he designs the pageants, and, with the aid of committees selected by him, makes all necessary arrangements for the production of the same. This gentleman, with singular taste and ability, has planned and supervised all the Rex processions that have adorned the city since 1875. He, together with Messrs Edward C. Hancock and Louis J. Solomon, organized the Rex organization in 1872, and he has since that time devoted much time and labor to bring it to its present state of perfection. Louis J. Solomon has the honor of having been the first King of the Carnival. Edward C. Hancock took a very prominent part in the forming of the Rex organizations and to him New Orleans is indebted for the beautiful displays of 1873 and 1874. Both he and Mr. Solomon are now residents of New York City. Major Eugene May, Captain H. M. Isaacson, Captain William H. Braughn, Captain William Pierce, Captain Charles M. Whitney and Messrs. Frank W. Baker. T. Geuerelly, D. M. Kilpatrick, W. I. Hodson, A. A. Maginnis. J. Bercegeay, Victor Tanner and a host of other prominent young citizens are hard working members of Carnival Court and efficient officers in His Majesty's service. They give their time and talents with as much devotion as if they were serving a real monarch or getting a salary equal to that of the President of the United States. Among the prominent members of the Royal Host of national reputation are U. S. Grant, General W. T. Sherman, Schuyler Colfax, Chief Justice M. R. Waite, Admiral Robert H. Wyman and Captain James B. Eads, who, under their respective ducal titles of America, Tecumseh, Indiana, Justice, Admirality and Engineers. show as much devotion and enthusiasm for the house of Rex as any of its more humble members. The costumes, including jewels, jewelry, arms, papier-mache, animals, etc., are made in the World's Emporium, Paris, and the decoration of floats and other details are attended to in New Orleans. The average cost of one of these pageants reaches the sum of thirty thousand dollars, all of which is paid voluntarily by the members of the two organizations. Another mystic society has been organized in New Orleans for the purpose of parading on the Tuesday preceding Mardi Gras. The society is called the "Krewe of Proteus" and composed of men of taste and unlimited means. From this it will be seen that the future visitor to New Orleans will be entertained for one entire week preceding Mardi Gras by the most beautiful pageants that money, talent and energy can produce. The parades of Proteus, Momus, Rex and the Mystic Krewe in one week present an attraction that no city in the world can equal.

www.ingramcontent.com/pod-product-compliance
Lightning Source LLC
Chambersburg PA
CBHW032001010726
47493CB00007B/2281